Your Child's Mind

Trusting God's
Design to Guide Your Child's
Development

Mary Ezzo M.D.

Solid Foundations Publishing

Acknowledgements

Many thanks are given to my husband Paul and my sons David and Matthew for their encouragement and support. Special thanks to my sister Jeanette Ezzo for countless hours of editing and help with research. Thank you to my prayer group and my friends at Cornerstone Church in Spooner, Wisconsin. I did not fully understand how much I needed our entire church family until God nudged me out of my comfort zone. Thank you for walking with me, praying with me and helping me locate resources for each part of this journey.

I would like to thank those people who generously shared their professional resources:
Beck Visual Communications for the illustration.
Dr. Harry Chugani: Wayne State University, for the use of his PET scan studies.
Tom Kelby at Hands to the Plow Ministries for his technical guidance and editing.
Earnie Larsen for the use of his teaching materials.
Dr. Dave Larson at the International Center for the Integration of Health and Spirituality for encouragement and access to his spirituality research.
Michael Macone for Cover Design.
Dr. Michael Phelps; UCLA, for the use of his PET scan studies and his lesson on brain development.
Dr. David Walsh at the National Institute for Media and the Family for generous access to his resources.

Solid Foundations Publishing
P.O. Box 41
Cottage Grove, MN 55016
651-458-3573

ISBN 0-9719476-0-0

Dedication

This work is dedicated to you, Lord Jesus.
I am a living testimony of your power to transform a life.
It is yours.

CONTENTS

Introduction

Our Lord has created in me an intense passion for children and parents. As a family physician, I am privileged to see unique aspects of life. I am invited into the lives of patients during times of suffering and pain. Frequently, I have the opportunity to know many of the members of a family; and I am able to see the impact the family has on the individual. Most incredibly, I get to watch children grow up. From that thriving newborn to the struggling teen, I can see the hand of God and marvel at His design.

The other area of my work that brings a unique aspect to parenting is the opportunity to understand the science behind the brain and behavior. The decade of the 1990s is frequently called the “Decade of the Brain” because medicine and science have seen an explosion of information in this area. I have been enthralled by all of it.

I want to bring this information to you. I think, as parents, if we can understand what actually happens in the brain, we can use that as a foundation for understanding God’s Word within the context of His design. I am not an expert in parenting or the brain. I have only pulled together the information. As Christians, God is our source of wisdom. My hope is that this information will give us a new framework where it will be easier to understand the promptings of the Holy Spirit as He guides us in our parenting. It will reinforce the way God has designed the body in total accordance with His laws.

This book began as weekend parenting seminars. From these seminars the following principles were gathered to be carried throughout this book. There is a method to the madness. We will start with a bigger picture of what's happening in society. From a cultural level, we will then explore what's happening in the mind and the spirit of the individual. We'll explore how tightly interwoven they are. We'll talk about particularly strong forces in derailing our children, such as anger, addictions and spiritual strongholds (thought processes that set themselves up against what is truth). We'll talk about our role as parents in that spirit-mind connection. We'll conclude by coming full circle and looking again at the larger culture. This time we'll look at our role in it.

Yes, the battle is intense. Unfortunately, the battle appears to be for the minds and hearts of our children. And it may get worse. We don't need another parenting book. We need to humble ourselves and come back to God as the source of our power. 2 Chronicles 7:14 says, "If my people, who are called by my name, will humble themselves and pray and seek my face and turn from their wicked ways, then I will hear from heaven and will forgive their sin and will heal their land." Let us cling to the Truth that God has given us! Anything that is not His Truth will be used by Satan to build strongholds in the minds of our children.

Here are the key principles:

1. **Trust God**. He is real. He is incredible. Much territory has been lost in the area of Christian parenting. Rebuilding the family and reclaiming our heritage with God will be much like Nehemiah when he rebuilt the walls of Jerusalem. We need, first as individual families and then as Church families, to assume our position on the wall and rebuild

what has been burned and destroyed. It will require vigilance, veracity and vision. It will require unity in the body of Christ. Nehemiah 4:14-18 says " 'Don't be afraid of them. Remember the Lord, who is great and awesome, and fight for your brothers, your sons and your daughters, your wives and your homes.' When our enemies heard that we were aware of their plot and that God had frustrated it, we all returned to the wall, each to his own work. From that day on, half of my men did the work, while the other half were equipped with spears, shields, bows and armor. The officers posted themselves behind all the people of Judah who were building the wall. Those who carried materials did their work with one hand and held a weapon in the other, and each of the builders wore his sword at his side as he worked. But the man who sounded the trumpet stayed with me."

2. **If we are going to rebuild with one hand and hold a weapon in the other, we need to understand and know how to use our assigned "weapons."** We need to have a working knowledge of the spiritual armor. We need to train our children to understand the armor as well.

3. **Prayer is an essential powerful privilege**. We desperately need the hand of God upon us and our children.

4. Brain development essentials:
    - **The brain is designed to imitate**. That's how it learns. Our children are watching

us live! They will imitate us. Who we are speaks louder than what we say. Who we are is defined by our relationship with our Lord Jesus Christ.

- **In the first 14 years of a child's life, brain development is constant.** The brain is laying down neural pathways that will be there for a lifetime. Interestingly, we have the same number of nerve cells from birth to adulthood. But, from age 3-4 until 10 years the rate that the brain is making neural connections is twice that of the adult brain. What we think is important has to be taught in these younger years when the brain is 'wiring up'. [1] If we abdicate our responsibility to train the brains and hearts of our children, the world will fill in the gaps. Every single experience that goes into the brains of our children will be registered somewhere. The neural networks that are used the most frequently will become dominant. That is why God tells us that teaching our children must be constant. When we continually model and teach His precepts they become the strongest and most dominant neural networks in their brain. First He designed the mind, then He instructed us in Deuteronomy 6:5-9 to "Love the LORD your God with all your heart and with all your soul and with all your strength. These commandments that I give you today are to be upon your hearts. Impress them on your children. Talk about them when you sit at home and when you walk along the road, when you lie down and when you get up. Tie them as symbols on your hands and bind them on your foreheads. Write them on the doorframes of your houses and on your gates." God designed these miraculous brains. He is trying to tell us that training has to be constant and consistent.

5. **We need to know how to access resources in our churches and in the larger Body of Christ.** There is a huge resource section at the end of this book. God is pouring His Spirit out through the body of Christ. Please access what He is making available to parents. Offer your gifts and talents to Jesus Christ to be used in service to His people.

6. **We need to practice skill in parenting that keeps our eyes focused on the real goal for our children, Jesus Christ**. Training our children to recognize Him as their destination in life is what parenting is all about.

7. **As parents, we need to remember that we are not alone**. We need to constantly remember that this incredible intense protective love that we have for our children is only a very small glimpse into the Greatest Love that willingly culminated on the cross.

May you be blessed and encouraged on this journey.

Mary Ezzo

CHAPTER 1

The MORAL and SPIRITUAL DEVELOPMENT of CHILDREN in this MEDIA AGE

The challenges to parents today are almost endless. Some of those challenges are external ones. They are the ones that distract us; but we feel some level of control in managing them. These are the challenges of fatigue and busyness. It is the challenge of a culture that has become antagonistic toward Christian values. It is the frustration of recognizing that our kids face pressures we never would have anticipated a decade ago. It is the whirlwind of the pace of this rapidly changing society. It is the challenge of learning to protect our family time by saying 'no' to the good things.

Surprisingly, for many of us, the real challenges to parenting are internal ones. They are the struggles that lie within our wounded hearts. They are the internal challenges and the silent unspoken lies within our mind. Those are the questions about our faith. We continually try to make sense of what we truly believe. We wonder what keeps us on the fence in our ability to parent from a basis of Christian Truth. Our culture teaches evolution and yet, a deeper longing in our heart compels us toward an awesome God.

Many of us are struggling with wounds from our own childhood. Parents who have been emotionally wounded as children encounter very unique struggles as they try to build healthy parenting patterns. Part of the purpose of this book is to bring hope that there truly is an answer to the pain and struggling.

Parenting today encompasses all of this. We are whole people. Regardless of the masks we wear, our struggles are not limited to the external. But, whether we enter parenting whole or wounded, we all have a growing awareness that the world is changing fast. We have the sickening realization that it intends to crush and devour our children.

The information contained in the following pages is meant to bring encouragement and renewed strength to those who feel God is a key player in their lives and in their families. The Christian home can and must remain a fortress in the midst of chaotic cultural times. The Truth that God has given to us through Jesus Christ and the prophets of the Old Testament can remain our cornerstone to raise and train our children with a solid foundation.

This is particularly important and difficult at this time in our life, because the predominant postmodern thought is openly antagonistic toward Christianity.

The processes moving us toward the postmodern mindset have been at work in the world for the past millennium. If we can understand the roots of our current climate of pluralism we can begin to see how and why God was removed from our mainstream culture. As parents, this will hopefully give us a fresh understanding of where we are today on the timeline of this spiritual and cultural battle. We need to understand how immersion in our culture affects us!

The most compelling purpose of this book is to bring us as parents back to our God and Jesus Christ as the source of power and wisdom in parenting. It is to help us understand that our struggles in believing God for His promises stem in part from what we have been indoctrinated as a culture to believe from our 'cultural elites' and great thinkers. Satan will use anything that is not God's Truth to lull us to sleep.

As we study the brain you will be able to see God's design and the relevance of God's Word in science. The current information on the way the brain learns and develops profoundly reinforces what God has been telling us all along about His incredible design of the body and mind. Hopefully, we will be able to apply these new ideas and concepts to our parenting. Most of this information we know at a deeper level because God prompts our hearts. The scientific information merely offers a new framework into which we can place our Christian beliefs and growth in His divine wisdom.

In a way, the science of the brain gives us new and convincing reasons to get off the fence and parent the way we feel compelled by the Holy Spirit. It gives us the courage to get off the fence and show up fully dressed for the battle for the minds of our children.

We, as a generation of parents, need to respond to the new and frightening information that the many forms of media dramatically affect the brain development of our children. We are starting to see huge accumulations of data that these exposures affect them significantly later in life. This is particularly true of violent programming. [1]

Above all, it is my prayer that this information will encourage struggling parents to willingly give God back a key role in their heart and accept His wisdom as the ultimate unchanging parenting resource. Let the power of the Holy Spirit set the goals He desires for our children. Let His power give us the courage and strength to stick to those goals.

Understanding the Spiritual Battle

The brain learns well through word pictures or metaphors. We'll use many metaphors because they make information easy to remember. The first one is used to answer the questions; "How can we prevent our children from being crushed by the world? How can we build resiliency and self esteem into our children?" Please be assured that most of the brain research we'll discuss later shows that the environment and parents are incredibly important in this area. We make a tremendous difference in the lives of our children. However, this is also where we need to introduce the spiritual battle.

For our metaphor, picture Satan holding two soda cans. The soda cans represent two children, their hearts and their minds. Now, you can picture him in any way you desire, but remember, the Bible is fairly specific that Satan aims to destroy. So you may want to capture his evil with anger and fury in your word picture. However, more likely in the lives of our children, he will look beautiful and deceptive, like an angel of light. They won't recognize him as the enemy. As Satan begins to tighten his crushing grip, he looks at the soda cans. One is full and sealed shut; the other one is empty.

As he squeezes, something very predictable happens. The empty can crushes easily down to nothing in his menacing hand. However, the full can is not easily crushed. This infuriates the beast, and he tries harder to crush the can. Whoa! See how powerful word pictures can become? We know there are many areas in which he is crushing our kids including their sexuality, Internet porn, addictions, and relativism. The list goes on and on. So we struggle as parents. How do we build our child's self-esteem? We start by making the commitment to fill their mind and heart only with the Truth. Anything that is not God's Truth, Satan will use to build strongholds in the minds of our children.

Dr. Craig Ellison reminds us of the true source of self-esteem. He writes, "Our appearance, achievements, or affluence will not give us a healthy, stable self-esteem. Instead these elements foster pride when we measure up; and depression when we don't. Galatians 6:3-5 grounds self-esteem in accurate, sober self-evaluation that does not involve comparison with others but in accurate assessment before God." [2]

We're all in a spiritual battle. Everyday it rages. We need to be aware of it. We need to fill the soda can by giving our kids true knowledge of our God. They need the knowledge of His character and His promises to be given a priority place in their developing mind. "The one who is in you is greater than the one who is in the world." (1 John 4:4) Empower them with this truth!

Ways to Empower Children to see that "The one who is in you is greater than the one who is in the world."

1 John 4:4

1) **Teach them the truth about God the Father.**
They are created with a unique and special purpose. God has a reason why they are here. He gave them a perfect mind and body for their purpose here. Teach them knowledge of His attributes. They will have to understand the character of God to know right from wrong later on. That is the only way to teach discernment. Moral judgments are right because they agree with the character of the Creator.

2) **Teach them the truth about God the Son.**
They have been given the Word of God through Jesus Christ. There is incredible power in that which has been given to us through Jesus. Teach them that they have a soul of tremendous worth. Remember, our mainstream culture tries to avoid conversations about the soul. Can we help them to understand that they are so incredibly loved that Jesus died for them? Can we model unconditional love to our children? Most children develop their concept of God by the love they receive through their parents. Can we prepare them for the role they play in the body of Christ? Can we start telling them about the Bigger Story?

3) Teach them the power of the Holy Spirit.
He is the one who will dwell within their soda can. He is real and He is a God-sent live-in counselor. We, as parents, can experience and know the unbelievable

power and comfort of the Holy Spirit. Our children can meet the Holy Spirit through us. But, they have to make the decision on their own to seal the can by inviting Him in to dwell as ruler of their hearts. Remember, God has only children, not grandchildren. Once He is given permission to seal the can, it is difficult to crush. He is the only source of real power in today's crushing society. Once the Holy Spirit is given permission to seal the can Satan can only crush a child if a child re-extends permission to Satan to do so. We need to remind our children that Satan has already been defeated. We'll talk more about this in the chapter on strongholds. Even if the world fills that soda can with its false wisdom it cannot seal the can. A can that is filled, but not sealed, will still be crushed. There is only one way to seal it and solidify its strength.

With this picture in mind, what is our role as the parent? Although we cannot control everything that goes into the developing mind of our child, we can do a tremendous amount. We can keep out what we know will give Satan an edge in the battle. We can talk to them and teach discernment about the things that the world is teaching so they can process it all within a context of Truth. This gives the world less power in forming the values and thought processes of our children. And we can pray for our Lord Jesus to cover them with His blood, His love and His protection.

Remember, the sealing of the soda can has to occur in the heart of your child. Only your child can ask for His divine presence. Our part is to help them understand the Holy Spirit. They need to see Him alive in our lives. Otherwise, teaching something abstract like the Holy Spirit is easily lost in media's competing technologies. They will be seduced by the counterfeits of fast-paced distractions.

Please, don't underestimate the power of the Holy Spirit in our children. We place such limits on what He can do! He is astoundingly alive and present in our world and in the lives of many children. It is not an impossible dream!

As a family doctor, I am frequently reminded that our time with our children is very short. We have a tremendous amount to teach in a short number of years. I am also astounded by the number of hours that children are permitted to watch TV or 'play on the computer' or 'surf the Internet'. We need to be using that time in a better way. We need to use the time we have with our children to teach them to face a very challenging culture. It's not by accident that they are alive during these complex times. We need to equip them for the battle.

BUBBLE WRAP

This leads to the second metaphor, Bubble Wrap! One of our tendencies as parents when the heat gets particularly intense is to pull back. We gather our children under our protective wings and 'bubble-wrap' them. As an immediate response this can be good parenting. In our current cultural times, throwing them to the wolves to develop their 'street smarts' is foolhardy. But, there is also a world of hurt out there. We have already spoken of the reality that many of the wounds to the heart occur as children. Could it be that Jesus Christ, as the head of His body on earth, wants to use our children in easing the wounds of other children?

Ron Hutchcraft changed my perspective as a parent in his book *The Battle for a Generation*. He made two very poignant points about our children. First he states;

> They need help standing back and seeing what's going on with their generation. They need to know that right before their eyes Satan is working overtime to produce a generation where the lost kids know nothing about Jesus and the found kids aren't living for Him – a generation he can finally own with his death and darkness.[3]

Secondly he explains;

> God has chosen them to live in this generation where the battle has grown more intense. God has chosen them to be on the front lines of the most important days of the battle. We can tell today's young people, 'we already know who has the winning power in the battle. The only way we'll lose is if you don't show up or if you surrender.'[4]

His words, both profound and sobering, give us a broader perspective on parenting our children. Our human tendency is to pull back and cocoon our children against the barrage of influences in the world. We fear that those influences threaten to crush them and certainly knock them off course from knowing God and accepting Him as Lord of their life. But, this is effective parenting only if we are using that time to systematically replace the bubble wrap with the armor of God. We can't keep them bubble-wrapped until adulthood. Our Lord needs them as much as He needs us in His body.

So our challenge as parents is to understand the armor and trust God. We need to pray for discernment as to how and when to 'release them' to be salt and light. We need to understand the developing mind of our children and rely on the mind of Christ. We need to understand the developing mind so we know **why** we need to keep certain influences out. We also need to understand the developing mind so we know **why** we need to repetitively bring certain influences in!

Ephesians 6:14-17 explains the spiritual armor of God.

"Stand firm then, with the belt of truth buckled around your waist, with the breastplate of righteousness in place, and with your feet fitted with the readiness that comes from the gospel of peace. In addition to all this, take up the shield of faith, with which you can extinguish all the flaming arrows of

the evil one. Take the helmet of salvation and the sword of the Spirit, which is the Word of God."

THE ARMOR OF GOD

Satan will use anything that is not God's truth to build strongholds in our child's thinking. It is important, therefore, to base all our teaching on the truth. The **belt of truth** lays the firm foundation in our child's developing mind.

The **breastplate of righteousness** is essential to give them a true sense of right from wrong. God's character is the unchanging source of what we know to be right and wrong. We need to teach them the trap of relativism and keep their **feet fitted with the readiness that comes from the gospel of peace**. This means they need a perspective that includes the fact that Jesus Christ wants to use them in His church here on earth.

We need to give them a **solid shield of faith** and help them to see God in the world. His Spirit is active in the world right now! We need to help them see that God keeps His promises. All of them! We need to let them be fortified by the faith stories they hear from us, at church and in letters from missionaries. The world wants them to think that their faith can't possibly be true. The world will confuse them with pluralism. It will accuse them of arrogance when they claim one true God. Don't let Satan crush our children. It is important to keep a dialog going that discusses the conflicting world's messages.

Fitting them with the **helmet of salvation** is giving them the mind of Christ. When Jesus beckons them, they would see the world with a unique compassion that is the mind of Christ. When they are tempted by the flesh, they would have the ability to turn from it and choose an intimacy that is much more rare and precious.

Finally, they will be ready to pick up the **sword of the Spirit**, which is the Word of God. In the Word of God there is more power than they could ever imagine.

In Ephesians 6:18 Paul concludes his explanation of the armor of God by saying, "And pray in the Spirit on all occasions with all kinds of prayers and requests. With this in mind, be alert and always keep on praying for all the saints." Interestingly, Paul doesn't say to put on the armor and 'go for it'. We must never forget prayer as a most important part of replacing the bubble wrap with armor. We need to cover our children and the children of this generation in prayer and prayer and more prayer.

Ultimately, the battle for the hearts and minds of our children has become so intense that the job we are doing as parents and grandparents has become the most significant task we will do in our lifetime.

Finally, it is my heart's earnest desire that we will become very determined as parents. Let us plant the roots of our parenting firmly in Jesus Christ who is the only "Solid Foundation." Let us learn to unabashedly trust the wisdom and truth of His Spirit. Otherwise, we will likely be crushed and knocked off course as frequently as our children. We need to be very solid in our convictions. We need to make a distinct choice for Jesus Christ and get off the fence. We need to reclaim our courage to be salt and light to the friends of our children and to hurting parents. They are being crushed without the hope that there is a way of triumph and not destruction.

We need God's wisdom to pass along our values in a deliberate way. Parents who elect to parent by 'default' now live in a culture that will flood their children with a quite different set of values.

Now is the time! NOW. In the story about Mary and Martha Jesus tries to tell us that we need to prioritize the time we have right now. We need to spend time with Him so that our own spiritual growth affords us the wisdom we need as parents. We need to take time with our children to shepherd them in the same way.

"The choice before us is plain: Christ or chaos, conviction or compromise, discipline or disintegration. I am rather tired of hearing about our rights and privileges as American citizens. The time is come - it is now - when we ought to hear about our duties and responsibilities of our citizenship. America's future depends upon her accepting and demonstrating God's government." [5]

Peter Marshall (1902-1949) Chaplain of the United States Senate.

"This is all the inheritance I give to my dear family. The religion of Christ will give them one which will make them rich indeed." [6]

The Last Will and Testament of Patrick Henry, November 20, 1798.

To My Grown Up Son

My hands were busy through the day;
I didn't have much time to play
The little games you asked me to-
I didn't have much time for you.

I'd wash your clothes, I'd sew and cook;
But when you'd bring your picture book
And ask me please to share your fun,
I'd say: "A little later, son."

I'd tuck you in all safe at night,
And hear your prayers, turn out the light,
Then tip toe softly to the door…
I wish I'd stayed a minute more.

For life is short, the years rush past…
A little boy grows up so fast.
No longer is he at your side,
His precious secrets to confide.

The picture books are put away;
There are no longer games to play.
No good-night kiss, no prayers to hear -
That all belongs to yester-year.

My hands, once busy, now are still.
The days are long and hard to fill.
I wish I could go back and do
The little things you asked me to.

Author Unknown

As parents, our time is now.
This is all the time we have been given.

CHAPTER 2

The SIGNS of the TIMES

**"Red Sky at Night; Sailors Delight.
Red Sky at Morning; Sailors take Warning."**

IS TODAY REALLY DIFFERENT THAN THE PAST?

Our temptation as parents, when Satan wants to quiet the swell of concern in our hearts, is to think that life today is not really very different than it was in the past. There were drugs and sexual promiscuity when we were growing up. Are things really changing as quickly and drastically as we are sensing? Where are we on the cultural timeline?

Jesus encourages us to be aware of the signs of the times. In Matthew 16:1-4 the unbelieving Pharisees and Sadducees asked Him to show them a sign from heaven. He said, "When evening comes, you say, 'It will be fair weather, for the sky is red,' and in the morning, 'Today it will be stormy, for the sky is red and overcast.' You know how to interpret the appearance of the sky, but you cannot interpret the signs of the times. A wicked and adulterous generation looks for a miraculous sign, but none will be given it except the sign of Jonah."

Do we know how to recognize the signs of the times? A few years ago I started speaking to parents about the effects of TV and different forms of media on the developing mind. During one family visit to my hometown, there were several generations of 'elders' present at our get-together. What an opportunity! I turned on the video camera and asked them to tell me about when TV was introduced to most households, what life was like, and how life changed. Above all (I told them) I wanted to understand how and why this country had moved so far away from God! America has Christian roots! What happened? The discussion that followed was invaluable. Our elders have such a tremendous amount of untapped insight.

Among the elders who grew up in the United States, they spoke of the depression and hard times. They told me about wanting to give their children what they never had and wanting to build a better life. From their painful memories I became aware that they never had the intention to "indulge" their children.

Then they described the 'Warren Court' when prayer was taken out of the schools as the deciding factor in the downfall of our country. I was struck by the powerlessness that they felt in the decisions of that court at the time.

Then quietly a voice piped up from the corner. Roger, my sister-in-law's dad, grew up in Canada where there was no Warren court. And yet, the same force was working in Canada at the same time taking God out of the culture. He talked about how hostile the attitudes of the Canadians were becoming toward 'going to church.'

Then, I happened to read one of David Barton's Wallbuilder Monographs explaining how the Judicial System moved away from being based in the Judeo-Christian code of ethics. He noted that:

> Following Charles Darwin's presentation of his evolution thesis in "Origin of Species" in 1859, Christopher Columbus Langdell, Dean of the Harvard Law School, theorized that as man

> evolved, then his laws must also evolve. Deciding that judges should guide the evolution of the Constitution, in the late 1800s he introduced the case law study method under which students would study judges' decisions rather than the Constitution.
>
> This method was quickly embraced by other law schools. As a result, by the 1920s, the ideas found in "Blackstone's Commentaries on the Law," the law book of the Founders and of American courts for well over a century, were discarded. "Blackstone's" was deemed to present an outdated approach to law because it taught that certain things were always wrong and did not change, particularly those related to human morality and behavior. Under evolutionary law (also called 'positivism' or 'pragmatism') nothing is absolute or transcendent; everything is changing. [1]

So, is the real culprit Darwin? His theory of evolution certainly caused a paradigm shift in the current thinking of the time. Yet Darwin was quoted in "Darwin on his Deathbed" as saying, "I was a young man with unformed ideas. I threw out queries, suggestions, wondering all the time over everything; and to my astonishment the ideas took like wildfire. People made a religion of them." [2]

I had the sudden realization that Satan will use for his purposes, anything that is not God's Truth. This is particularly true if the climate in the minds and hearts of the people in that cultural time is ripe for it. It took many slow cultural processes to change human hearts since the testimonies of early Christians. How could hearts change so radically? These were the same hearts that met the person of Jesus Christ in the flesh. They witnessed the Holy Spirit's power personally. What happened to lull us to sleep? How did we finally conclude as a culture that we evolved and in fact there is no God in the picture at all? The theory of evolution would not likely have taken hold in the hearts of early Christians.

Many things have transpired that changed hearts. It was not just Darwin or the Warren court. When TV was first introduced it would have met with certain demise if it were originally filled with the pollution it chokes our children with today. No, we had to be lulled to sleep as a culture before the changes could happen so effortlessly.

I was a young man with unformed ideas. I threw out queries, suggestions, wondering all the time over everything; and to my astonishment the ideas took like wildfire. People made a religion of them.[3]

Charles Darwin

WHERE ARE WE ON THE TIMELINE?

It is here that we'll attempt to rebuild the timeline and reconstruct what happened to prime the hearts and minds of Americans. Hopefully, this information will paint the bigger picture for our current world as parents. There have never been prior times like this in history. Dr. Richard Swenson, in his book *Margins*, suggests we are truly living in unprecedented times. Life has never been this fast or tumultuous. We live from one crisis to the next. He states;

> We are immersed in a crime and prison crisis; a drug-abuse crisis; a national debt and inter-

> national trade deficit crisis; a savings and loan and banking crisis; a health care system and Medicare crisis; a sexually transmitted disease crisis; a liability and litigation crisis; an ethics crisis at every level of personal and public life; and the inexorably deepening environmental crisis. Our families are relentlessly torn apart by divorce, abuse, incest, and teenage pregnancies. Our educational system remains woefully deficient. Inner cities are war zones. Breakdown on a large scale is now within our reach.[4]

Dr. Swenson later quotes child psychologist David Elkind who explains;

> "Social supports have been bowled over by progress. Although affirming relationships are probably the single best protector against stress induced damage, we live in an impersonal world. Study after study confirms that a healthy marriage, family and community support structure yield better health and increased longevity- a kind of buffering system against the pain of distress." [5]

It is interesting to review the graphs in the Appendix of Dr. Swenson's book. Starting at about 1960 we saw an exponential increase in information, complexity, and change. We saw exponential rise in bankruptcies, bank closings, costs of housing and health care costs. We also are in the midst of a huge increase in mail and junk mail. [6]

In a recent review in American Psychologist the authors note "...violence in the United States began to increase fairly dramatically in 1965, exactly when the first generation of children raised on TV began to reach the prime ages for committing violent crimes." [7]

A little later we'll see how directly these high stress levels affect our immune systems and the levels of brain chemicals that determine our thinking. For now, let it set the stage that it is not our imagination that life seems just a little out of control. It's not our imagination that we just solve one parenting issue and get broad sided by the next. It's not our imagination that the speed of life is exponential. But how did we get here? Why did God choose us for these days?

There are key changes that seemed to shift our cultural beliefs and take God systematically out of the picture. When a shift is so large that it totally changes the direction of our thoughts it is called a "paradigm shift." Interestingly, this was anticipated. Deuteronomy 8:13-14 warns, "and when your herds and flocks grow large and your silver and gold increase and all you have is multiplied, then your heart will become proud and you will forget the LORD your God…."

THE WAYS WE SEE AND EXPERIENCE GOD

We're going to try something a little challenging here. We are going to walk through the timeline by using a diagram of the human body. We'll show how each way that we see God has been blinded by a different **paradigm shift.**

To do this let's establish a few key ways that we see and experience God. Then we can look at how each of these has been taken from our culture. It will be our visual metaphor. The form of a human person will be our backdrop to tell the story. Remember, as you look at this image of man, that there is a spiritual battle for this human being. Evil needs the use of the human person to infuse it with power. God desperately loves His creation and wants fellowship with him. Jesus Christ desires to use our hands for His purpose here on earth. There is a profound spiritual battle that underlies this timeline. The battle is for the heart and mind of man.

How do we learn to see God?

(1) We know Him through divine revelation. This is where He communes with us directly, teaches and guides us. Sometimes this is via direct revelation and sometimes it is through the way He directs our thoughts as we read His Word. This is where He wants parents to be! He wants us to trust Him for our wisdom. This concept seems a long way off to many parents. Our loss of the illumination of His divine revelation arises from a culture that has taught us that it could not be real. Those feelings of doubt are also part of living in a culture that sees divine revelation as invalid because it cannot be seen or measured. They are an indication of the way we have been lulled to sleep.

FAMOUS PEOPLE WHO UNDERSTOOD DIVINE REVELATION

Surprisingly, many famous people understood and experienced divine wisdom and revelation.

Abraham Lincoln was pressed by many differing opinions during the Civil War. Yet, he relied on his own revelation from God. He asserted;

> I am approached with the most opposite opinions and advice, and that by religious men, who are equally certain that they represent the divine will. I am sure that either the one or the other class is mistaken in that belief, and perhaps, in some respects, both. I hope it will not be irreverence for me to say that if it is probable that God would reveal His will to theirs on a point so connected with my duty, it might be supposed He would

> reveal it directly to me; for unless I am more deceived in myself than I often am, it is my earnest desire to know the will of Providence in this matter. And if I can learn what it is, I will do it. [8]

George Washington Carver (1864-1943) helped to revitalize the economy of the South after the Civil War with his breakthroughs in agriculture. He relied on God alone in his laboratory. He never took textbooks in with him for his experiments. He explained it this way,

> God is going to reveal to us things He never revealed before if we put our hands in His. No books ever go into my laboratory. The thing I am to do and the way of doing it are revealed to me. I never have to grope for methods. The method is revealed to me the moment I am inspired to create something new. Without God to draw aside the curtain I would be helpless.[9]

Several of our past presidents relied on this revelation.

> There are a good many problems before the American people today, and before me as President, but I expect to find the solutions to those problems just in the proportion that I am faithful in the study of the Word of God.[10]
>
> President Woodrow Wilson, 1923

> America seeks no empires built on blood and force. No ambition, no temptation, lures her to thought of foreign dominion. The legions which she sends forth are armed, not with the sword, but with the Cross. The higher state to which she seeks the allegiance of all mankind

> is not human, but of Divine origin. She cherishes no purpose, save to merit the favor of Almighty God. [11]
>
> President Calvin Coolidge 1925

We also see God through the beauty of His creation. I stand in awe when I contemplate the wonder of the human body, the intricate design of the heart valves or the majesty of a Christmas Cactus. I can see God everywhere as I walk through the woods or along a beach. The workings of the molecules of the human body are an exquisite orchestration. Each molecule is a perfectly fitting key for a lock somewhere in the body. The human lungs are branched like trees on the inside of the body and each little branch has an air sac at the end that uses oxygen and puts carbon dioxide into the air. Meanwhile in nature, God created trees with a leaf at the end of each branch to use the carbon dioxide and turn it back into oxygen. Creation is filled with the presence and evidence of God.

Unfortunately, most of our children now reside in cyberspace and see very little of God in their world.

We also experience God in the fury (the Beast) of His world. We come to rely on God and His strength and His mercy during our times of trial and suffering. We feel His tender arms during our times of loss. We feel His healing power during times of illness. We heal under His forgiveness when we fail as parents. Suffering doesn't mean God has abandoned us. Rather, it gives us an arena to experience Him in profound ways. Isaiah 42:25 also says, "So he poured out on them his burning anger, the violence of war. It enveloped them in flames, yet they did not understand; it consumed them, but they did not take it to heart."

Now let's look at that diagram. The picture of the man on the following page is labeled to show how we see God. The numbers correspond to chronological dates on our timeline that mark when those specific areas of the human person had been won by Satan. Or, put more precisely, it shows how the specific ways that we see and experience God have been lulled to sleep. What we live with we learn! We have been taught and trained by our "cultural elites." Those are the men and women in power that have the ability to define and pass down our culture.

The heart of man is depicted centrally in the picture. The place we give God in the center of our being determines everything our body will do. All our actions are based upon what resides in our heart. God has designed and reserved that spot for Himself. If we replace Him in our heart, Satan has access to use the tremendous spiritual force within our human person. We are the one's that can infuse evil with power!

Once the human spirit is lulled to sleep and no longer recognizes God's voice as Truth, it becomes vulnerable and is tossed about by the teachings of man. In fact, we have hardly noticed that Satan has handed us the sword of postmodernism to carry. He has instructed us to carry the sword of his anger and aggression in our current cultural times. God designed us to carry the sword of His Spirit.

Please understand that God has not ceased to exist. He has not abandoned us. We have rather closed down our ability to see Him and sense His life-giving presence. Isaiah 28:15 says, "You boast, 'We have entered into a covenant with death, with the grave we have made an agreement. When an overwhelming scourge sweeps by, it cannot touch us, for we have made a lie our refuge and falsehood our hiding place."

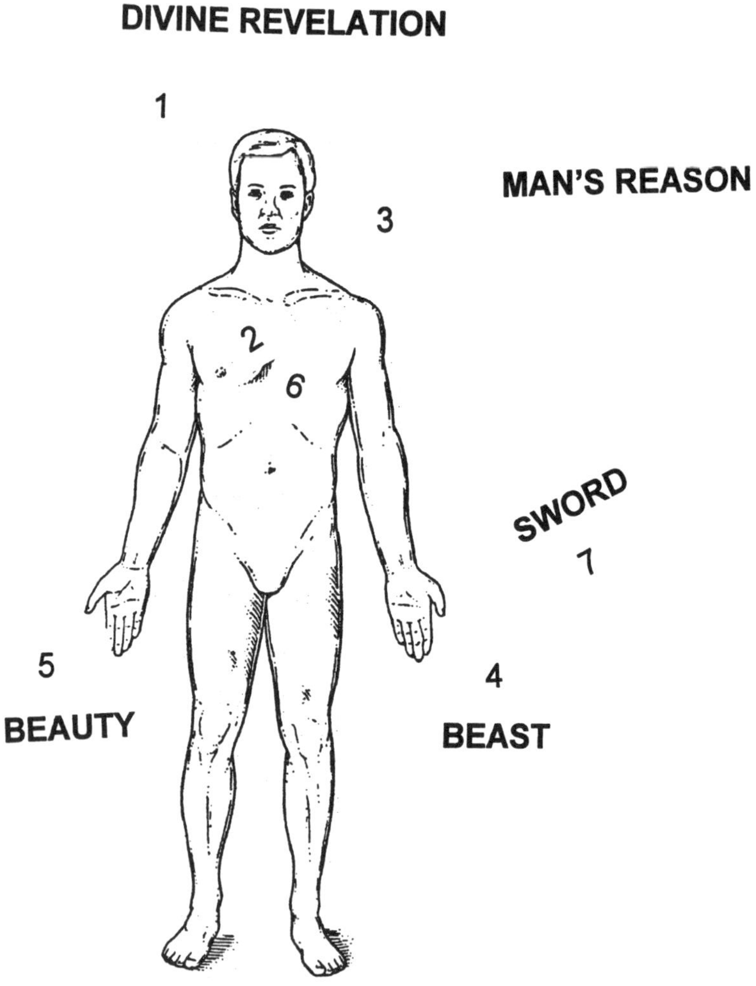

Illustration courtesy of Beck Visual Communications

Body Timeline shows the chronology of how our ability to see God has been changed by our culture.

(1) **Man started to believe that human philosophies were equal to divine revelation. Thomas Aquinas 1200s** "The grass withers and the flowers fall, but the word of our God stands forever." Isaiah 40:8

(2) **Humanism placed "man" on the throne of the heart; replacing God. Renaissance 1300s –1600s.** "They exchanged the truth of God for a lie, and worshipped and served created things rather than the Creator-who is forever praised." Romans 1:25

(3) **The Age of Enlightenment placed Man's Reason as the way to know truth. 1700s** "You turn things upside down, as if the potter were thought to be like the clay!" Isaiah 29:16

(4) **The Industrial Revolution provided man with sufficient technology for him to rely on himself for solutions to disease and nature's fury.1700s-1800s.** "Woe to those who go down to Egypt for help, who rely on horses, who trust in the multitude of their chariots and in the great strength of their horsemen, but do not look to the Holy One of Israel, or seek help from the LORD." Isaiah 31:1

(5) **Evolution declared that there was no creator. All the beauty of the world was an accident. 1859.** "Shall what is formed say to Him who formed it, 'He did not make me'? Can the pot say to the potter, 'He knows nothing'?" Isaiah 29:16

(6) **Modern Times replaced "self" of the throne on man's heart. Satisfying the flesh became paramount. 1850s – 1990s.** "Everyone who is called by my name, whom I created for my glory, whom I formed and made." Isaiah 43:7

(7) **Our current postmodern world has become a culture of anger and aggression; particularly toward the things of God.1990s to current.** "In repentance and rest is your salvation, in quietness and trust is your strength, but you would have none of it." Isaiah 30:15

UNDERSTANDING THE TIMELINE

Let's start our timeline with the **Roman Empire.** "Christianity became the dominant religion of the Roman Empire early in the 4th Century. For the next 1000 years it dominated philosophy and tolerated little opposition." [12] Most of our American thought comes from western Europe. It is from ancient Greece and Rome that many philosophers emerged, such as Plato, Socrates and Aristotle. It was into this thriving Roman culture that Jesus Christ chose to appear in history as the Word of God.

The Christian Church grew rapidly despite great opposition. When the Roman Empire collapsed somewhere around 500 A.D., the Church stood in the gap as a unifying entity in Europe. Interestingly, many of the teachings of the ancient philosophers such as Aristotle (384-322 B.C.) were lost with the fall of the Roman Empire.

This collapse of the Roman Empire ushered in the **Middle Ages** in the 5th century. During the Middle Ages Artists focused on glorifying God and they willingly assumed humbleness and anonymity. [13]

Somewhere around the 13th century the Islamic scholars discovered and translated the teachings of Aristotle into Latin. Averroes completed this translation and "gave teachers access to his scientific works and to his logical method of argument... The scientific writings prompted research into the natural world.." [14] These new teachings seemed to suggest that truth was independent of revelation. This seemed to push the first domino.

To the church leaders at the time, this was a very alarming shift in the cultural thinking. The writings of Aristotle are very well written and convincing. They are, however, not based on the teachings of God. Somehow they had to find a way to reconcile this reintroduction of Aristotle's teachings with those of the church.

This became the task for St. Thomas Aquinas (1225-1274). He successfully merged the teachings of many different philosophies from Aristotle, Islam, Judaism and Christianity. His followers became known as Scholastics. He accomplished the integration of the wisdom of Greece and Rome with the wisdom of Christian thought. [15]

As we have seen, there was an enormous amount of cultural pressure on Aquinas to accomplish this task. However noble the intent of the process, it managed to give Christ's teachings an equal footing with the teachings of secular philosophers in our Christian Worldview. Now, the teachings of the Bible and the teachings of non-Christian philosophers were both considered correct and accurate. This marks the number (#1) on the diagram with the demotion of divine revelation as equal to man's reason.

By the end of the Middle Ages there seemed to be more distortion of God's truth. Understandably, once we tried to blend the world's teachings with those of Christ, the power of the teachings of Christ started to lose their authority. The authority of the church then started to wield more power than the teachings of the Bible.

THE RENAISSANCE

The Renaissance began in Italy around the 14th century and continued until the 16th century. People of this time again began looking at their roots in Roman Civilization. This time in history is notable for its outstanding accomplishments! They subsequently adopted a system of thought called Humanism where the worth, unique talents, and potential of the individual person is paramount. Compton's Encyclopedia gives it this slant: "The Spirit of Humanism tried to free society from the bonds of ignorance and superstition in which it had languished for a millennium." [16]

When your herds and flocks grow large and your silver and gold increase and all you have is multiplied, then your heart will become proud and you will forget the LORD your God

Deuteronomy 8:13-14

Fame and the regard of other men became important. It was a time known for the availability of education to people of all walks of life. It specifically focused on the 'here and now' and concrete sensory answers. Through Humanism "Man" was given a key place on the throne of the human heart. This is the number (#2) on the diagram where God is replaced by 'man.'

It was this trend that eventually gave rise to the Protestant reformation in the north of Europe at the same time as the Renaissance in the south. Two key men were prominent at this time. John Wycliffe (1320-1384) was angered by the church for their selling of indulgences, pilgrimages and its strong veneration of the saints. He argued that only the Bible could be the supreme authority. He was grieved at the practice suggesting that man could buy salvation. He translated the Bible into English to make it available to ordinary people. John Huss (Jan Hus: 1369–1415) pleaded for the return to the teaching of scripture. He felt man could only return to God through the work of Christ. Huss was executed as a heretic in 1415. [17]

About this time, the availability of education to ordinary people during the Renaissance was allowing for many discoveries. Remember, in 1492 Columbus arrived in America and started the exploration of a New World.

THE REFORMATION

By the 1500's things began to change. Martin Luther posted his list of 95 suggested reforms against the Catholic Church in 1517. By 1520 the Protestant Reformation was underway in the Northern part of

Europe. "At it's core, therefore, the Reformation was the removing of the humanistic distortions which had entered the church." [18]

> "They took seriously that man needs the answers given by God in the Bible to have adequate answers not only for how to be in a open relationship with God, but also for how to know the present meaning of life and how to have final answers in distinguishing right and wrong. That is, man needs not only a God who exists, but a God who has spoken in a way that can be understood." [19]

Ultimately, the Reformation ended the supremacy of the pope and the religious unity of the people. It established protestant churches.

It is worth reiterating the ways in which the infiltration by humanistic thought – growing over the years but fully developed by 1500 - showed itself.

First, the authority of the church was made equal to the authority of the Bible. Second, a strong element of human work was added to the work of Christ for salvation. Third, after Thomas Aquinas there had come an increasing synthesis between Biblical teaching and pagan thought. [20]

Schaeffer, *How Should We Then Live? The Rise and Decline of Western Thought*

THE ENLIGHTENMENT

This time in history was followed by "The Enlightenment" or "The Age of Reason." These cultural times are exactly what they sound like. Scientific discoveries emphasized the accomplishments of men through their ability to think and reason. It was a time dominated by the "belief that the world and humanity could be rationally studied and explained." [21] During this time of our culture, men became very impressed with their ability to give life meaning all on their own. Josh McDowell in his book *Right from Wrong* insightfully adds:

> While the Renaissance mind acknowledged God (but removed him from the throne, so to speak, replacing Him with man), many leaders of the Enlightenment (such as Voltaire and Descartes) claimed that if there were a God who had created the world, He had no contact with it now - which meant that men and women were left to discover truth on their own; they could expect no help from God. Man had to depend upon his powers of reason if he hoped to discern the truth. Standards of right and wrong were not based on the nature and character of God; they were the products of human reasoning. [22]

So, God was taken off the throne during the Renaissance and man replaced Him (Humanism). Then during the Enlightenment we decided we didn't need Him for revelation and meaning and insight and wisdom. This is the number (#3) on the diagram where "man's reason" replaces Divine Revelation as a way to know Truth. It is interesting to look at the hundreds of years needed to accomplish this process.

THE INDUSTRIAL REVOLUTION

During the Industrial Revolution (1700s –1800s) man became capable of incredible accomplishments. The inventions and innovations during those years were unprecedented. Man became impressed with what he could accomplish and didn't need to rely on God any longer. Men learned to trust that they could solve problems with their own intellect and their technology and inventions.

"You may say to yourself, 'My power and the strength of my hands have produced this wealth for me.' But remember the LORD your God, for it is he who gives you the ability to produce wealth, and so confirms his covenant, which he swore to your forefathers, as it is today."

Deuteronomy 8:17-18

The Industrial Revolution marks the (#4) on the diagram when we no longer needed to rely on God to help us with the "Beasts" of nature.

Consequently, in 1859, Darwin presented his ideas when the world was ready to accept his queries as fact. Sadly, by embracing evolution, we abandoned even the ultimate Truth that we are created and found a way to remove that last remnant of God from our cultural thought. This is the number (#5) on the diagram where we are no longer able to see God in "Beauty."

The Warren Court didn't start the process. It just delivered another blow to God in our worldview. Now we are able to recognize at least in part why parents are struggling with the ability to recognize and experience God. He has been squeezed out of our culture systematically over the previous 1500 years.

MODERN TIME

Finally, we close in on modern times. The actual timeline date for the modern age is after the Reformation. "...the Reformation has been called a turning point in history. It ushered in the Modern Age because, once the people's religious unity was destroyed, they began to think in terms of their own regional interests." [23] Much of our thinking still borrows from late 18th century Romanticism. This era arose as a rejection of Enlightenment. "Romanticism exalted intuition, feeling, inspiration, and the genius of human creativity."[24] This thinking highly values the self. "The Supremacy of the individual is not the whole of Romanticism, but it is pivotal." [25]

Compton's Encyclopedia explains:

> The pushing aside of reason also challenged centuries-old accepted values and standards. It suggested that there are no objective values that need to be accepted by everyone. The individual, in tune with his feelings, becomes the determiner of values and thus can attempt to reorder the environment according to personal understanding. [26]

However, at this point in the story we see the lives of children start unraveling at a very rapid pace. By the 1850's factories existed and the workers were very poor and children suffered. The children of the poor received no education.

Our culture later experienced two World Wars, including the horrors of Hitler. We hosted a civil rights movement and a feminist movement. We saw federal control begin in our public schools. Kids in modern times began living lives of broken homes, school violence and addictions. The lives of our children became remarkably stress filled. We'll talk about the consequences of that stress in later chapters.

In 1859, when Darwin introduced his theory of evolution in his thesis *Origin of the Species*, the main tenet of evolution became that "Man is improving, ever moving upward, continually progressing." [27] Our children somehow never found that culture Darwin promised that was ever improving. Instead, the tremendously high stress has created a surge in disease and problems.

And what about the Warren Court? How did our country ever give a court of law so much power? It took many years for judges to bring this new concept of case law based on the belief of evolutionary justice into widespread acceptance. However, the court's ability to bring about actual changes in society was evident in profound ways in the Warren court of 1950s.

David Barton explains,

> Warren's announcement in Trop v. Dulles (1958) foreshadowed what was soon to become reality. In that case he explained, 'The Constitution must draw its meaning from the evolving standards of decency that mark the progress of a maturing society.' Under Warren's guidance and during his tenure, the Court completed its transition into a powerful societal force, striking down long-standing practices such as school prayer and Bible reading while openly acknowledging that it was doing so with no precedent.[28]

Read this twice. This concept is very important to recognize as Christian parents.

The sexual revolution in this country also has a deeper root than the 1960's. Families moved to cities during the industrial revolution. Cars became available for dating. Havelock Ellis wrote his controversial books at the turn of the last century. His "Studies in the Psychology of Sex" written from 1897-1928 was at first considered pornographic. [29] He started introducing ideas suggesting that marriage lasts only as long as love endures. He introduced ideas about trial marriages and no fault divorce. The scene was being set for the sexual revolution before the 1960's. [30]

Over time, our bustling cities became a melting pot of

differing lifestyles and values. Then in the late 1940s 'Media' with its immense capacity to tell the stories of the culture, started to redefine us as a society. The culturally elite were no longer just the philosophers and great writers. Now, our TV and movie-makers became the most powerful of the cultural elite. And at a very fast pace, the values of our movie-makers started to restructure the thought processes of our culture. Unfortunately, as we will learn as we study the brain, what we learn from our culture, we also become! Shortly after the introduction of TV we saw technology multiply and entered the exponential part of our timeline.

Somewhere in the timeline we became a nation that consumes rather than produces. Our public schools started emphasizing the social sciences rather than the hard sciences. Families became more fragmented with less of a chance for them to tell their own story, and therefore, less of a chance to pass down their own values. Families became immersed in that proverbial boiling pot of a rapidly changing culture. Families became less and less aware of how far society actually had traveled from representing the values they believed. Cultural indoctrination is this process of taking the values of a culture and making them part of your own personal beliefs. Many times, this happens without our conscious thought. We learn to imitate and recognize as familiar that which surrounds us.

For Christian parents, immersion in a changing culture is a very powerful force to reckon with.

It takes a full-throttle 'about face' to pull your family out of the pot and redirect them in the direction of your Christian values.

Modern man placed "self" on the throne of the heart with the number (#6) on the diagram for "Self." At this time in history we began focusing on satisfying the self and the desires of our flesh.

THE POSTMODERN ERA

Finally, in the last 5-10 years or so, there has emerged the Postmodern Era. The emerging theme of our contemporary world has become relativism and the ability to set our own moral code. In a belief system of relativism, all truth and morality is dependent on the context. We decide what we want to believe as a culture. There is no absolute truth. Although the Supreme Court in 1963 ruled against it, the religion of secularism has become deeply entrenched. They wrote, "The state may not establish a religion of secularism in the sense of affirmatively opposing or showing hostility to religion; thus preferring those who believe in no religion over those who do believe." [31]

It doesn't seem to matter what the Supreme Court ruled. We are on a runaway train. We are parenting in the midst of this developing postmodern thought. It is coalescing into its tornado-like form as we live each day. Dr. Cameron Lee defined postmodernism in Christian Counseling Today. He explained, "The quote [about postmodernism] on page 16 is drawn from the fourth edition of Irene and Herbert Goldenberg's Introductory Family Therapy Textbook, published in 1996. The second edition, published in 1985, has no parallel passage. What I am calling the "Postmodern turn" in family therapy is a late development." [32]

We are parenting in unprecedented times, and perhaps the greatest challenge of postmodern thought is its new tolerance. What frequently comes from this viewpoint is hostility toward anyone, like a Christian parent, that has a unique point of view. As in the Supreme Court ruling above, it lashes antagonism out toward those who believe in the Christian religion, but embraces those who believe in no religion. Interestingly, we'll see in the last chapter that this thought closely parallels the religious beliefs of our TV and moviemakers! The open antagonism is a new change in our culture unique to the postmodern mind. That is the final number (#7) on our diagram where the sword is added to the picture. It is the sword of hostility, anger and rage. It is Satan's weapon that he has handed to us while we were lulled to sleep.

Dr. J.P. Moreland tries to provide a context for this hostility when he writes, "Postmodernism leads to the institutionalization of anger. Post-modernists are preoccupied with power struggles that surround language use and social practice, and they see themselves as part of a missionary movement to liberate powerless, oppressed victims from dominance." [33]

As I work with Junior High School students they explain to me that their peers call them arrogant if they speak of their Christian values as though there could be one sole Creator. Look at how far we have come from 1894 when Ohio Governor William McKinley wrote, "There is no currency in this world that passes at such a premium anywhere as good Christian character...The time has gone by when the young man or the young woman in the United States has to apologize for being a follower of Christ." [34]

PLURALISM

Our current day culture certainly expects our children to apologize for their love of Jesus Christ. The only acceptable belief–system to the postmodern mind is pluralism. Pluralism has become not only acceptable and honorable, but also expected. There is no "One Supreme Creator" in the postmodern mind. There are hundreds of equally acceptable gods. How do we train our children to understand this type of hostility toward their beliefs from their peers? Can we begin to understand how intimidating this postmodern culture will be to our children who really want to conform and be like their peers while at the same time wanting to be loyal to the God they have grown to know and love? Sure, we can bubble wrap them and keep them in a Christian subculture with like-minded Christian hearts, but there is a world that is perishing out there. There is a generation of kids being devoured by the hate. Our Lord Jesus is calling our children to something so much greater than bubble wra

> **But by making power struggles and victimization a central focus of the post-modern crusade, the movement dignifies anger by institutionalizing it and placing it on ideological high ground, and it creates anger by fostering relational suspicion according to which there is a victimizer under every linguistic tree. America is a country of very angry people, and post-modernism is to be blamed for its share in creating this situation. [35]**
>
> Doctor J. P. Moreland

So where did this postmodern thought come from? We'll discuss that more completely with the research data in the last chapter on "Who's telling the stories." However, briefly, postmodern thought very closely parallels the spiritual belief systems of our TV producers and movie–makers. It parallels the belief systems of our cultural elites. It does not parallel the beliefs of the majority of Americans. Please understand the power of those elites in our culture. What we live with under their teaching and guidance we will learn. The thoughts that we are constantly exposed to in our environment will be what our brain learns and believes!

CULTURAL IMMERSION

Immersion in a culture and the desensitization that

occurs with 'cultural indoctrination' is not a new phenomenon. Harriet Beecher Stowe's plea to the American people in her concluding remarks of *Uncle Tom's Cabin* in 1851 was a plea against cultural immersion and its desensitization to the evils of slavery. Abraham Lincoln said of her book, "So you're the little lady who started the big war." [36] Mrs. Stowe writes movingly about the problem of slavery and the responsibilities of Christians during those days. Remember, this is about 8 years before Darwin released his theory of Evolution. She is pleading to a culture that has already fallen asleep. Read closely what she writes and try to understand the power of cultural immersion as you read. She writes;

> But, what can any individual do? Of that, every individual can judge. There is one thing that every individual can do, they can see to it that they feel right. An atmosphere of sympathetic influence encircles every human being; and the man or woman who feels strongly, healthily, and justly, on the great interests of humanity, is a constant benefactor to the human race. See, then, to your sympathies in this matter! Are they in harmony with the sympathies of Christ? Or are they swayed and perverted by the sophistries of worldly policy?[37]

That sounds like something we might write today! The same concerns are evident. She is sounding the trumpet to those that have been lulled to sleep by the current culture.

Her final concluding paragraph reads;

> A day of grace is yet held out to us. Both North and South have been guilty before God; and the Christian Church has a heavy account to answer. Not by combining together, to protect injustice and cruelty, and making a

> common capital of sin, is this Union to be saved, but by repentance, justice, and mercy; for, not surer is the eternal law by which the millstone sinks in the ocean, than the stronger law, by which injustice and cruelty shall bring on nations the wrath of Almighty God! [38]

Let's talk one more moment about immersion because it is a phenomenon that keeps many Christians immobilized and sitting 'on the fence.' Immersion is the concept of being deeply involved or absorbed in our culture. A commonly used metaphor is the frog in boiling water. He is not 'sensitive' to the changing temperature of the boiling pot. He boils to death. Our culture is our boiling pot.

> **Cultural immersion is an all consuming hold of culture as it becomes the source of thinking and feeling in its members. So engulfing is this power that we cannot discuss the essential theme of our culture at its crossroads without being locked into it ourselves. We are in it, and we are hard pressed to find a fulcrum outside of it with which to leverage a shift. [39]**
>
> Ravi Zaccarias, *Deliver us from Evil*

> **I believe the majority of the silent majority, young and old, will sustain the loss of liberties without raising their voices as long as their own life-styles are not threatened. [40]**
>
> Francis Schaeffer *How Should We Then Live? The Rise and Decline of Western Thought*

CHAPTER 3

INSIDE the MIND

Now comes a huge leap. We have to move from the macrocosm of the larger culture to the world of tiny molecules in the brain. Sometimes, trying to explain the complexity of the brain is overwhelming. Reading the mass of books written about the current research can be confusing because discoveries are happening quickly, and information is, therefore, outdated just as rapidly. I am not a neuroscientist. Much of my knowledge of the brain comes from reading the research of those that are neuroscientists. I will simply try to rephrase it in practical terms and information for you as parents. The brain is fascinating. But, the reason we need this information as parents is to help us understand the "WHY" part of why we teach our kids and the "HOW" part of how they learn.

THE CENTRAL NERVOUS SYSTEM

The easiest way to understand the brain and the nervous system is to use the metaphor of a flower. The brain has a spinal cord and brain stem much like the stem of a flower. It has important life-giving parts that cluster in the middle like the stamens and pistils. It has the six lobes of the cerebral cortex that are like the petals. What happens in the lobes of the cortex determines all the unique characteristics and fragrances of the human flower. Think for a minute of all the different kinds of flowers you have seen; their uniqueness and beauty. Even the most inconsequential violet is enormous in its beauty.

The brain is the same way. Our genes, in combination with our experiences, create petals that are unique to us. Our personalities and behaviors are the net result of the cortex.

Let's try to do the neuroanatomy. It's not hard. It's just a lot of new words. However, if this chapter seems overwhelming just skip it for now. It's here to return to later if you need it as a reference.

The basic building block of the brain is the nerve cell or neuron. The **neuron** consists of a cell body and long fibers at each end. The end that receives information from other nerves is called the **dendrite.** The dendrites form a huge tree-like expanse of connections. There are hundreds of dendrites per nerve cell. (They look like the branches of a tree.) Dendrites make proteins and amino acids that will become the chemical messengers for that cell. The part of the nerve cell that sends a message out from the cell body is the **axon**. This is the transmitter part of the nerve. It works to transfer the chemicals down the nerve cell once they are made by the dendrites.

First key principle: Inside the nerve cell the dendrites receive information and the axons transmit information.

Glial cells are 70-80% of the brain. They hold all the nerve cells in place and keep the brain environment healthy for the neurons to work. Glial cells actually make some of our immune chemicals. These cells wrap themselves around neurons to form a **myelin** sheath. This acts as insulation for the nerve cell and helps increase the speed that messages travel along the nerves.

Astrocytes are brain cells that maintain their ability to proliferate throughout life. When neurons die these Astrocytes fill in the space in the brain. They pick up chemicals that the neurons release and transform them back into a usable form for the nerve cells to use over and over again.

Another concept that you will read about is brain **'plasticity.'** This is the ability of the brain to change and mold itself. Cells that are 'plastic' are uncommitted to a permanent neural network. We now know that some remodeling and relearning goes on throughout life. Interestingly, nearby nerve cells in the cortex can actually learn to do their neighbor's job in the event of injury. And, even more surprising information suggests that stem cells can step in and repair parts of the injured brain! We'll discuss in the chapter on addictions that neurons can increase or decrease the number of receptors or the amount of neurotransmitter as a way to self-regulate.

The most amazing thing about nerve cells is that they never touch! They talk to each other by releasing chemical transmitters from the end of the axon. These chemicals flow into a gap between the nerves called a **synapse.** Once they are in the synapse, the chemicals, called **neurotransmitters**, find the exact place on a nearby dendrite where they fit perfectly (like a lock and key). A different process of enzymes in the synapse then inactivates the neurotransmitters.

Second key principle: Neurotransmitters are released from the ends of nerve axons and have a perfect lock and key fit with a receptor site on the dendrites of another neuron. This is how the nerves talk to each other.

Understanding these neurotransmitters will make sense as we talk about the different concepts like anger and the effects of music. For now, all you need to know is that they are usually divided into two groups. Small molecules are small amino acids. The most important ones are **Acetylcholine** (Ach), **Dopamine** (DA),

Norepinephrine (NE), **Serotonin** (5HT), **GABA**, and **Glutamate**. [1]

The second group is called **neuropeptides** and these are made in the cell body. They are mostly released from the hypothalamus and the pituitary gland. This process involves transcribing genes in the nerve cells. These are the **opioid peptides** like B-endorphins, enkephalins and dynorphins; the **pituitary peptides** like ACTH, and the **gastrointestinal peptides** like Insulin. Opioids are the most studied and they play a role in the behavior response to pain and stress. [2] We think these chemicals also play a role in the euphoria of the sexual response.

Acetylcholine is most important at the muscle-nerve synapse so we won't talk much about it. It is also important in the parasympathetic nervous system.

Glutamate is released from at least 50% of the nerve cells. It acts as an **excitatory neurotransmitter**. When it binds to a NMDA receptor on the dendrite of a nerve cell it opens the calcium channels of the neurons. This starts the **action potential** (electric current) running down the nerve cell. This is the key process in Long-Term Potentiation and memory. **GABA** is an **inhibitory neurotransmitter**. Interestingly, **GABA** is synthesized from **Glutamate** with Vitamin B6 as an essential cofactor. It prevents the neuron from being able to get excited. It does this by opening the Chloride channel in the nerve cell and this keeps the action potential low.[3]

Third Key Principle: Glutamate is an excitatory neurotransmitter; GABA is an inhibitory neurotransmitter. Glutamate turns nerves on. GABA turns nerves off.

Tyrosine, one of the amino acids in our diet, is manufactured into Dopamine and Norepinephrine. These are also called Catecholamines. Dopamine and Norepinephrine are made in the synaptic vesicle just before they get released at the ends of the axons. These transmitters are degraded in the synapse by MAO Inhibitors (enzymes). These are the chemicals released with stress or flight or fight responses.[4]

Now that we understand the nerve cell, let's try to understand a basic structure of the way they are arranged in the brain. The physical structure of the brain is just the arrangement of all these nerve cells. Most scientists call the physical structure of the nerves the brain. They call the processes that the brain performs the mind.

Most of neuroscience divides the brain into a **central nervous system** and a **peripheral nervous system**. The **central nervous system** consists of the **brain**, and the **spinal cord**.

The **peripheral nerves** are those nerves that go out from the central processing center into the body and connect to the organs like heart and lungs, the muscles, and the blood vessels. In addition to communicating with the body through the peripheral nerves, the brain also connects and communicates with all the parts of the body by **hormones and peptides** that are created in the brain. Amazingly, this means that the brain sends commands to the body through both nerves and chemicals that it releases into the blood. In this way, a body part is able to get a message through a telephone line (the peripheral nerves) or by postal mail (hormones that somehow know how to get to the proper address.)

GRAY MATTER FORMS CONTROL CENTERS IN THE BRAIN

Scientists also talk about gray and white matter. To understand this, we have to look back at that simple nerve cell which is composed of a **cell body** with a long **axon** (the output fiber) and many branching dendrites (the input fibers). The **gray matter** of the brain is simply the nerve cell bodies in collection. Nerve cell bodies sit in layers across the top of the cortex (lobes of the brain). Remember that the genes are inside the nucleus of the cell body. They contain all the commands for that nerve cell. **Gray matter (cell bodies)** also form **control centers** in the brain when they cluster in small groups called **nuclei**. These control center nuclei lie in the stamen and pistil part of the brain 'flower' mostly near the center. Only the emotional control centers lie in the cortex. But even those hug the center of the brain closely.

These are important. Scientists have offered us much hope in treating disease by our new understanding of these control centers. The nerve cells that release Dopamine cluster in an area we call the reward center. They control pleasure and rewards; and therefore, addictions. The Dopamine centers are located in two areas; the Substantia Nigra and the Ventral Tegmental Area. These areas send connections to the basal ganglia (movement area affected in Parkinson's Disease) and to the medial prefrontal cortex (controls emotion).

Fourth key principle: Dopamine in the Ventral Tegmental Area controls addictions.

All Norepinephrine (NE) containing nerve cell bodies are contained in the brainstem in an area called the Locus Ceruleus. These nuclei send connections everywhere because this is one of the alerting neurotransmitters. It is released as a result of the fight or flight responses in the body.

These are critical nerve cells because when the level of catecholamine activity (both Dopamine and NE) in a particular brain circuit is decreased we see depression. When the nerve pathways get overstimulated we see schizophrenia or mania. For example, drugs that block the DA receptors are used to treat schizophrenia. In Parkinson's Disease the DA neurons are degenerating in the Substantia Nigra. So the disease is treated with medications that resemble Dopamine itself. With addictions, there is increased DA activity in the Ventral Tegmental Area.

Fifth key principle: Norepinephrine is the key flight or fight neurotransmitter.

Serotonin (5HT) is synthesized from tryptophan, another common amino acid in our diet. The nerves that make serotonin are found in the Raphe Nuclei in the brainstem. These nerve cells send axons out to the pre-frontal cortex (emotional center), to the thalamus and hypothalamus processing centers, and to the spinal cord. There are more than 12 types of serotonin receptors unique to different areas of the body. Serotonin regulates mood, sleep and wakefulness. There are around 40 known neurotransmitters and possibly another hundred that scientists are investigating.

Sixth key principle: Serotonin is a key neurotans-mitter for mood and behavior.

The cortex, or thinking brain, makes up the petals of the flower. It is currently divided into six lobes.[5]

1. **The Frontal lobe** controls motor function, motor control of language, emotion, discernment, and moral decision-making. This part of the brain develops most rapidly later in a child's life starting about age 7-8. This lobe has no direct sensory input into it. This incredibly important lobe of the brain relies on associative pathways it forms from the neural networks that are laid down in early childhood. It is therefore essential to be aware of what we are putting into the developing mind of our children.
2. **The Parietal lobe** contains the somato-sensory cortex and is an association area. This means it recognizes touch, vibration, hot, cold etc. It is essential for touch and spatial understanding. It is the connecting area for sight, sound and touch.

3. **The Temporal lobe** is the primary auditory cortex, it processes language comprehension and a higher order processing of visual information when meaning is attached to what we see. It contains the olfactory (smell) cortex and relays its information to the limbic system.
4. **The Occipital lobe** is devoted to vision.
5. **The Insular lobe** is responsible for taste as well as some cardiovascular, pulmonary and gastric functions.
6. **The Limbic cortex** is located deep inside the brain where the 'petals' fold over themselves near the brainstem. It is located along the rim of the corpus collosum deep in the midline. It runs along the medial surface of frontal, parietal, and temporal lobes. The parts of the limbic system are the cingulate gyrus, the hippocampus, the amygdala and the prefrontal cortex. The cingulate gyrus controls emotional expression and the hippocampus controls memory. We will talk later about the amygdala. This is a cluster of small nuclei tucked under the temporal lobe at the end of the limbic system. It affects the emotions directly and connects to the thalamus and the prefrontal cortex.

THE CORTEX OF THE BRAIN

Dr. Jane Healy, in her book *Endangered Minds* explains that;"The cortex is the control panel for processing information at three levels:

1. **Receiving** sensory stimuli
2. **Organizing** them into meaningful patterns so that we can make sense out of the world
3. **Helping** association patterns to develop abstract types of learning and thinking.

These later-developing 'association areas,' so critically important for planning, reasoning, and using language to express ideas, are the most plastic of all; their development depends on the way the child uses his or her brain at different stages of development." [6]

The Thalamus is a relay station for all the messages on their way to the cortex. Every sensory system of the body uses the thalamus. It also controls consciousness and sleep.

The hypothalamus maintains body temperature, regulates food and fluid consumption, and receives and sends information from all the endocrine glands of the body. It also controls reproduction and maternal behavior. This part of the brain acts to release the hormones that act in all of the other parts of the body. The brain controls the exquisite dance of hormones in the body.

Eric Jensen in his book, *Teaching with the Brain in Mind* describes fascinating parts to our learning. He states that,

> Bruce McNaughton at the University of Arizona discovered that a rat's brain activity patterns in REM match the patterns of the daytime learning session. (Lasley 1997) He suggests that during sleep time, the **hippocampus** is rehearsing the learning sent to it by the neocortex. This 'instant replay' consolidates and enhances memory.[7]

Development of the physical structure of the brain is called **'hard-wiring'**. This is the shape we see on a CT or MRI scan of the brain. New research shows that the physical structure of the brain actually changes with the way it is used! However, a large majority of how the brain develops is in the genetic make-up of the person. Interestingly, in 1808 Franz Joseph Gall proposed a science called Phrenology which believed that the shape of the bumps on the head could determine character and personality.[8]

> "Of course, experience – even different kinds of learning – changes children's brains," I was told again and again. If

> children's experiences change significantly, so will their brains. Part of the brain's physical structure comes from the way it is used.[9]

Now let's try to make sense out of all this basic information. The base of the brain contains the control centers from which our behavior originates. This is the same area that we have called the stamens and pistils part of the flower. The importance of this more central part of the brain is that it has the ability to shut down higher thinking processes if the person perceives danger. It is felt that this part of the brain is the center of instinctive behaviors. It is designed for those decisions that require us to 'think fast' rather than 'thoughtfully consider.' Now, remember we talked about all those nuclei and where they went? If the child is asked to respond quickly, the pathways simply bypass their connections with the cortex and give an urgent command to the body before we have a chance to think about it. It saves time in an emergency situation.

THE NERVE CELL IS THE BUILDING BLOCK OF ALL LEARNING

What we need to know as parents is that the more frequently we use a neural pathway, the more deeply it will become a part of the thought processes of our child's mind. Part of intelligence comes from building a dense network of dendrites and neural connections. The goal of healthy brain development is to build large numbers of dense nerve connections. These develop based on use and movement. Even late into life, it has been shown that nerve networks develop better if they are associated with movement in the body.

These synaptic connections are where learning begins. The more often a pathway is used, the more complex and thickened (like the branches of a tree) the connections become. If an area of the brain is not used, those nerve cells die off.

Each stimulus through the senses requires a response from the brain that builds up these dendritic connections. So the experiences we provide to our children make a difference.

The brain needs to be stimulated and the timing is very critical. We know in medicine that we must diagnose early any disease of the eyes in a baby that might prevent the retina from being stimulated by light. If the nerve cells of the retina are blocked from receiving light by a tumor in the eye, a congenital cataract or an eye that wanders and lets the sister eye 'see', blindness will develop. Remember that nerves that are not stimulated will atrophy. In this case, atrophy happens in the nerves of sight.

The more work the brain does, the more it becomes capable of doing. [10]

The key to getting smarter is growing more synaptic connections between brain cells and not losing existing connections. It's the connections that allow us to solve problems and figure things out. [11]

Scientists think that every neuron forms about 1000 synapses, and these groups of nerve cells are organized into local circuits. The thinking brain, for example, has very specific tasks assigned to specific areas. These are called neural networks. When the brain is injured by trauma, stroke, tumor or infection, there is a very specific function that is lost corresponding to the area that has been injured. That is why different kinds of injuries or diseases cause different losses in a patient.

The blood supply to the brain and the nutrition and fluids it brings to those brain cells is essential! Our children need plenty of good nutrition, not junk, to help build healthy brains. The brain will work best with plenty of good clean water. We don't think about that much. We need to physically feed their little bodies so that the brain has every opportunity to find what it needs for growth and development. Most parents figure out very quickly that a hungry child is irritable. A tired child is irritable. This is because the nerve cells are being asked to function without the basic tools it needs.

LEARNING DISABILITIES

We are not going to discuss much about the genetics of the brain, but that area is exploding with new information. Scientists are learning that our environments very distinctly affect which genes get turned on and expressed in a person.

When there is a learning disability, Jane Healy describes that;

> Although the young brain covers up to the best of its ability, small, unrecognized injuries or malformations probably are a factor in the subtle difficulties of many learning-disabled children. The problem is often not neurologically identified by current methods, but children and parents become frustrated because certain types of learning take longer when they must be accomplished by pathways less efficient than those originally scheduled to do the job [12]

That is why working with children with learning disabilities frequently and persistently consists of building, through repetition, more efficient neural pathways. If the genetic make-up of a brain does not allow for the most efficient circuit to develop, we try to work with the circuits that are there to make them more efficient. Computer technology has been a blessing in some of these areas where it can slow the spoken word down by milliseconds making it more discernible to the brain! Then, once the brain learns to hear and recognize the sound at a slower spoken rate, it lays down neural networks that become more efficient with use. Gradually, the brain won't need speech to be slowed down to discern the subtle differences.

A CHILD'S BRAIN LEARNS THROUGH ACTIVITY NOT PASSIVITY

Dr. Jane Holmes Bernstein described one of the most fascinating experiments to Jane Healy.

> "She describes a famous experiment in which identical-twin kittens were put in a large circular container painted with black and white vertical stripes – their only visual stimulation during a critical period of visual development. One kitten rode in a small basket that was attached to one end of a revolving balance beam. The other kitten was in a second basket attached to the opposite end of the beam; his legs, however, protruded from the basket. As he walked around, the beam revolved and his brother got a free ride. Both, of course, had the same visual stimulation of the vertical stripes. Later, it was discovered that visual receptor cells in their brains had developed differently, even though each had experienced the exact same scenery. The kitten that merely rode along was functionally blind for vertical lines! Only the kitten who had his feet on the floor, knowing where he was, aware of his position on the floor relative to the lines, developed those connections! Experience shapes brains, but you need to interact with the experience." [13]

Recognizing the need for movement, let us ponder these statistics. "In 1960, the average two-year-old spent an estimated 200 hours in a car. Today's two-year-old has spent an estimated 500 hours in a car seat." [14]

Here is another attempt to give a perspective to what our busy hectic lifestyles are doing to our children. Consider how neural networks are formed in our children. Passive activities will not build the complex neural networks they need. They need to be free to walk and crawl and explore their world. They need motor stimulation for the brain to learn.

We need to set solid limits on the amount of passive time in front of a screen that we allow our children. Not only is it preventing the development of a rich network of dendrites, but it also introduces values and images that the developing mind is not equipped to process.

NEUROTRANSMITTERS AFFECT MOOD AND BEHAVIORS

1. SEROTONIN

Antonio Damasio is very highly regarded for his research in the areas of emotion. He explains what they have found regarding serotonin.

> One of the roles of serotonin in primates is the inhibition of aggressive behavior (curiously, it has other roles in other species). In experimental animals, when the neurons in which serotonin originates are blocked from delivering it, one consequence is that the animals behave impulsively and aggressively. In general, enhancing serotonin function reduces aggression and favors social behavior.[15]

The key concept to remember here is that when serotonin levels are low, behavior is characterized by more depression, agitation, and impulsive aggression. When serotonin is high (too high) the person has more of a tendency to think obsessive-compulsively and to be more fearful and shy.

Our consistent parenting and the stability in our homes

affect the neural pathway development of our children. It leads, as we discussed above, to thicker dendritic synapses. Is it therefore also creating a network of more serotonin receptors? On the flipside, does the unlimited exposure to violent programming and a chaotic home life create a different cluster of synapses and sparser serotonin receptors on nearby dendrites? Or does it raise other chemicals to be dominant in the brain?

Michael Raleigh's research in monkeys suggests that:

> in monkeys whose behavior is socially well tuned (as measured by displays of cooperation, grooming, and proximity to others), the number of serotonin-2 receptors is extremely high in the ventromedial frontal lobe, the amygdala, and the medial temporal cortices in its vicinity, but not elsewhere in the brain; and that in monkeys exhibiting noncooperative, antagonistic behavior, the opposite is true. [16]

Serotonin seems to be an essential player in regulating the neural connections for emotions and drives.

NEUROTRANSMITTERS AFFECT MOOD AND BEHAVIORS:

2. NOREPHINEPHRINE

We also know that the neurotransmitter, **norepinephrine**, seems to be in an opposing position to **serotonin**. Scientists study norepinephrine when they try to understand the behavior of criminals. High levels of norepinephrine are found in impulsive crimes, and low levels of norepinephrine are found in premeditated crimes. Why might this be so? Remember, Norepinephrine is the brain transmitter that is high with stress and the fight or flight response. Dr. Bruce Perry at Baylor University feels that a component of this criminal behavior happens when the nerve cells that respond to norepinephrine actually start to burn out from being stimulated so continuously.[17] [18] We understand this process at the receptor site for glutamate and would propose that a similar process may work with Norepinephrine.

We think that the way that nerve cells die from too much neurotransmitter at the dendrite is like this. With glutamate toxicity, for example, the increased amounts of glutamate cause excessive stimulation at the dendrites. The calcium channels open to start the action potential. But there is a tremendous influx of calcium and this also activates calcium dependent proteases in the dendrites. Proteases are enzymes that produce free radicals and start to breakdown the actual plasma membrane of the neuron and the small structures of the cytoplasm of the cell. Consequently the neuron dies. Much of this happens in the brain with high stress hormones.

This phenomenon of nerve cell death is concerning because it explains how the criminal mind changes from that of being hot-blooded and impulsive to cold-blooded and premeditated.

MYELINATION

When a pathway is particularly important and regularly used, the brain wraps glial cells around that axon. This insulation with glial cells is called myelin. Once the myelin forms around an axon, the axon becomes very fast at transmitting impulses and doesn't allow other nerves to interrupt its action potential. Myelin coats a pathway, so to speak, so that there are no interruptions along the way. Myelin prevents interference.

Myelin seems to form in the innermost parts of the brain before the outside, and from the back of the brain before the front. The developing brain myelinates from the top of the spine (which are the arms and head) before the bottom (which are the feet and legs). That's why babies can reach before they can run.

WHAT IS UNIQUE ABOUT BRAIN DEVELOPMENT IN ADOLESCENCE

While many of us know of the rapid rate of brain network development in the first seven years, Dr. Harry Chugani's work shows that there is tremendous growth and development of the cortex in the adolescent years [19].

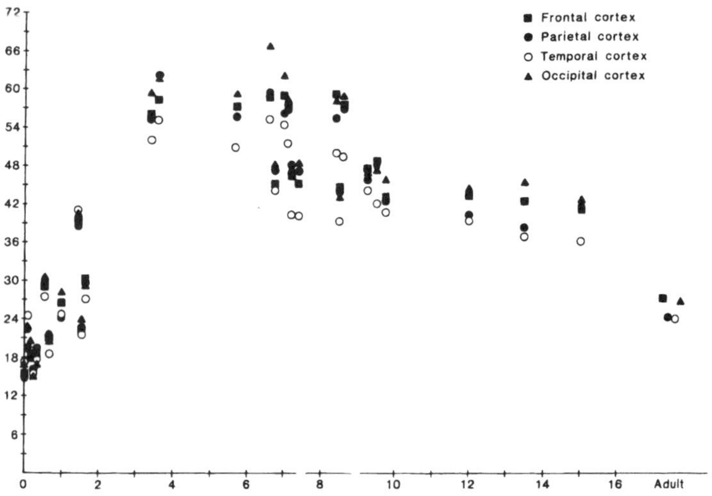

Absolute values or LCMRgic in cerebral cortex plotted as a function of age in normal infants and children, and corresponding values in seven normal young adults
Reprinted with permission from Dr. Harry Chugani [19]

This graph shows the rate of cortex (the thinking bain) development of our children. Please especially note that the frontal cortex depicted with a square has a high rate of new neural network development until it starts to fall off around age 16 or so. This is the part of the brain that does moral decision making as one part of its functions.

Remember that the prefrontal cortex is the part of the brain adolescents are developing when they start being able to think more abstractly. This is what they develop when they make moral decisions. This is when they develop their ability to plan and organize. They develop a sense of "self" and social conduct. The prefrontal cortex is developing right alongside the sex hormones becoming active. Therefore, adolescence is the time when the critical brain pathways for moral decisions; sexual response and sexual attitudes develop. Remember, during these years the prefrontal cortex develops by building associations from everything the child's brain has learned in earlier years. There is no direct sensory input into the prefrontal cortex. So, all of the impressions of right and wrong and of a sexual self that have been connecting since birth will be called on to make sense at this point in development.

Earnie Larsen, an internationally known speaker, tries to teach this concept this way. He states:

> "What we live with, we learn;
> What we learn, we practice;
> What we practice, we become, and
> What we become, has consequences." [20]

Everything we have painstakingly attempted to teach our children will start coming together and making sense as the prefrontal cortex develops. All of the foundation we have laid down in those little neural networks will start paying off. That is why Proverbs 22:8 says "Train a child in the way he should go, and when he is old he will not turn from it."

Early learning assists the development of the pre-frontal cortex and moral attitudes in adolescence. Dr Jane Healy explains:

> In the normally developing brain, prefrontal areas probably become active soon after birth but aren't truly operational until sometime around ages four to seven, with a spurt of myelination near puberty which may continue into adulthood. Unlike other cortical lobes, they do not have a direct "window onto the world"

for sensory reception, so their development builds on the sensory connections formed in earlier years and on the child's inner thoughts, language, and attempts to make mental connections. [21]

DEVELOPING EMOTIONAL INTELLIGENCE

There are many critical times in the developing brain. In the first year of life, experts believe that a child develops their emotional intelligence or their ability to relate to others and their world. [22] The process of attunement with the primary caregiver is particularly critical during this first year. How we respond back to our babies gives them the cues to build neural circuits in this area of emotional intelligence. We are constantly giving them cues about whether the world is a safe place or a fearful place. We give them the cues about how to feel about experiences by how we respond to them. Every life situation has emotions wrapped around it and we teach our children how to process this.[23] We'll discuss emotional intelligence in chapter eight. If a child grows up in a chaotic or abusive home environment a process called 'wounding' happens to the child rather than the development of healthy emotional intelligence.

CHAPTER 4

EFFECTS of TV and MEDIA: TEACHING DISCERNMENT

When our children are young, they need help laying their neural networks. They need to understand and explore the 'whys' of how the world works. This is a key time to keep them away from TV. It is also a time when spiritual truth has to be laid as part of the foundations. We'll discuss later, in the section on discernment, that it is very difficult to teach right from wrong if a child has no concept of a God or of this incredible process of creation. As we explore the world with our toddlers and young children, we need to keep God as part of the explanations and help them to build a consistent truthful worldview.

With that in mind we'll pull together a small amount of the vast research on the effects of TV and media on the developing mind. One of the best resources in this area is The National Institute on Media and the Family.[1] They have videotapes available to teach parents at schools or churches. The National Institute on Media and the Family has devised a curriculum to be used in the elementary grades to start teaching this information to students such that they become co-participants in monitoring their media usage. They encourage parents to develop a well thought out plan for how your family will use media and has information to do this. They have available brochures with down to earth ideas on how to "Tame the Tube" and establish a solid plan in your home for how you could handle media. Focus on the Family also has a video titled Mind Over Media as a resource for parents in this difficult area. It is geared to older children as part of their Life on the Edge Curiculum. (See Video Resources)

In the brain, most of TV speaks to the emotional centers. The emotional centers are both in the medial-frontal cortex and in the midline nuclei like the amygdala. Remember from Mr. Chugani's graph, that the higher cortical structures aren't fully developed yet. They don't start developing until around 7 or 8. Therefore, TV, which is very passive, almost forces the brain to receive instruction into the parts of the brain that are developed; and those are the emotional centers. This means the emotional centers are receiving instruction from TV before the prefrontal cortex has developed sufficient neural connections to teach discernment. TV has a very significant impact on the brains of young children.

HOW DOES THE BRAIN PROCESS INFORMATION FROM THE TV?

Sensory images from a television set enter the brain through the senses. The rapid pacing of shows grabs the attention of our children. The change in sound volume grabs their attention. Whatever way the TV stimulates the child, it is the thalamus that receives the message from our senses. From the thalamus the information is relayed to the amygdala to have an emotional response placed on it. The amygdala will determine just how quickly the brain needs to respond. The amygdala decides whether to stimulate the flight or fight nerves and release Norepinephrine. If this happens the body will increase the heart rate and start to release stress hormones. It also is responsible for creating the startle response.

Ultimately, our emotional centers will determine what we will remember and consider important. The amygdala has direct connections with the prefrontal cortex. So, if there is time, and if the prefrontal cortex has developed adequately, the emotional response can be processed rather than stored in memory circuits in the amygdala. Gloria DeGaetano in, *Grow Smart Brains Toolkit* notes: "Feelings and emotions arise before much actual thinking can take place about the visual input." [2]

David Walsh at the National Institute on Media and the Family describes the role of emotion quite graphically. He says, 1) Emotion focuses the attention of the brain. (Most forms of media deliver us an 'emotional jolt' to get our attention. The most common emotional jolts are violence, sex and humor. 2) Emotion is a major determinate of what we remember. 3) Emotion is a basic part of attitude. (Violence, for example, when it is constantly viewed creates an attitude of disrespect). 4) Emotion helps to motivate us. 5) Emotion is a stronger motivator for behavior than knowledge. [3]

Ultimately, one of the reasons we need to protect our children from extremely fearful and emotionally charged experiences is because their cortical function doesn't develop well until later in childhood. Simply stated, turn off the TV. It is far more educational to have them exploring their world and creating their own neural network connections and the meaning behind the experiences. Motor pathways in the brain have to be developed over and over to become healthy and complex. Turn off the TV. Stop the continuous bombardment to their attention center of the brain. Let them have lots of large motor experiences and fine motor experiences. Remember, our children need lots of real life experiences!! Jane Healy explains "Middle childhood and early adolescence are the most critical times to firm up automatic skills before the child is besieged with higher-level processing demands." [4]

TV AND MEDIA

Following is a collection of statements from experts in the field for you to think about when you make your personal decisions about screen-time that you will allow your children. This includes TV, Gameboys, video games, computer games and Internet use that you will allow your child . All of this information is from the brain development perspective, and it takes into account the ability of TV and media to teach as well as entertain. Remember, the experts are emphasizing that media, among other things, prevents the development of other aspects of the brain.

Eric Jensen, a pioneer in his advocacy for protecting the brains of our children, states, "Many scientists and researchers say they would ban television for all children before age 8. (Hannaford 1995). [5] Mr. Jensen later explains his reasoning when he states, "Television provides no time for reflection, interactions, or 3-dimensional visual development." [6]

In the video *Jolts and Tricks*, Dr. David Walsh explains that the real purpose of TV is to sell eyeballs to advertisers. If a TV show can keep us watching, it will have higher ratings. And higher ratings mean they can charge more to advertisers. In order to keep us watching, they need to keep us from getting bored. They have to continually jolt our emotional attention centers. They need to keep grabbing our attention. [7]

However, the child's brain learns better if it is allowed to complete a task. If TV is on in the background, the child's attention will be jolted intermittently to focus on the TV. This can prevent the child from developing the orderly neural network that would build naturally if allowed to find a problem and solve it through play. Instead the process of learning through play will be wrapped in frequent distractions and diversions from the screen. They need to be allowed to build their neural networks. We are raising a generation of children that is programmed to need these frequent stimulations and diversions. How are today's teachers ever going to be able to meet the expectations for thrills and frills that our children are learning to expect?

Many of the pioneers in the scientific world that try to warn parents of the effects of media do so with school learning in mind. Basically, they encourage us as parents to know the content of the media our kids use, to monitor the amount of time they use the different forms of media, to be consistent and to educate ourselves to recognize the effects of media on our kids.

Dr. David Walsh also developed "The Seven Building Blocks for School Success." He includes as one of those seven building blocks the ability to pay attention. That impacts how successful our children will be in school. [8]

A CHILD'S BRAIN LEARNS BY COMPLETING TASKS WITHOUT BEING INTERRUPTED. THIS BUILDS ATTENTION SPAN.

THE DEER ANALOGY

When I teach parents up here in the great northwoods about this concept of "the attention centers of the brain," I use the analogy of a deer feeding in a field. What that deer really wants to do is eat that grass. What your child really wants to do is pay attention to one activity for as long as it takes him to complete that neural network. However, if there are fast paced distractions in the room, like TV or video games, it will keep diverting attention away from the task at hand. A deer looks up with warning alarms in place for each activity he perceives in his peripheral vision or hears in the field. He really wants to eat the grass but will soon run off because his attention center has been called to action. Your child will not finish that neural network with his attention center continually being stimulated to respond to what is on a screen. And it may happen that the neural network that does develop is one that is in constant need of stimulation because that is what the child has just laid down! Kids need to touch, feel and manipulate their world. Turn off the TV and let them play!

When we discuss this concept of turning off the TV during parenting classes, most parents openly admit that life gets harder for the parent for a while. Our children have grown accustomed to being entertained. And the parent may have grown accustomed to that built-in babysitter that was keeping the home peaceful and quiet. Take heart! Our children soon learn to entertain themselves again, but it may take several weeks. As parents let's also try to remember that raising our children will take our time. It will take large quantities of time. They are worth it. The other option is far from optimal.

"Manipulations of 'arousal mechanisms' that separate brain and body may be related to reports from psychologists and teachers that today's children are increasingly 'touch starved'. A heavy diet of vicarious viewing that replaces real sensory involvement is directly antagonistic to the most basic principles of a young child's learning. Much early development of physical and mental skills – and of their foundations in the brain – comes from experimenting and solving problems with real-world materials. The long-term outcomes of forcing children's attention unnaturally may have even more serious implications than we have realized." [9]

Gloria DeGaetano notes: "Internal control of the attention span diminishes as the child becomes a spectator. When this happens for hours every day throughout early childhood, the likely outcome is a rambunctious brain, a brain that will most likely find it difficult to learn how to read and write." [10]

It should be remembered that although the brain may be distracted by the lights and action of TV it is really the repetitive and the familiar that brings them comfort and a sense of security. It is their sense of the familiar that lessens their stress and buffers them from the assaults of the world. This becomes important when we talk about the high stress levels of our children in a later chapter.

Jerking children's attention around may cause a certain amount of emotional withdrawal, as well. Young children, while involuntarily captured by novelty, really need repetition and familiarity. Anchoring experience in this way helps them gain a sense of organization and mastery. [11]

Jane Healy tries to alert parents to the way TV can negatively affect attention. She writes, "Three effects on learning abilities, all related to attention, have been suggested: 1) some television and videotape programming artificially manipulate the brain into paying attention by violating certain of its natural defenses with frequent visual and auditory changes (known as saliency); 2) television induces neural passivity and reduces 'stick-to-itiveness'; 3) television may have a hypnotic, and possibly neurologically addictive, effect on the brain by changing the frequency of its electrical impulses in ways that block active mental processing."[12]

When I do school physicals at 7th and 10th grade, I will frequently ask the child if they would ever consider media to be significantly violent that they would turn it off. I have yet to have any child say yes. When I ask "Why not?", they will frequently tell me that they know it is not real."What would you say if I told you that your brain thinks it is real?" They can't comprehend that even for a moment!

Although there is no movement present in the room, the brain perceives movement on the screen to be similar to threats in the environment. "Television is psychologically arousing, confirms Dr. Byron Reeves of the Department of Communications at Stanford, who conducted studies of viewers' electrical brain activity. Their brains did, indeed, respond to movement as though it were actually present, causing the nervous system to prepare for a physical response. Personally, Reeves told me he also believes these habits show up in school, as children become habituated to 'surprise and circus-type' presentations." [13] This becomes key in understanding the way media affects behavior.

Research clearly shows, however, that better students tend to watch less. Moreover, as viewing goes up, academic achievement scores eventually go down...They found that television's negative effects on reading skills were particularly strong for the more advanced abilities needed for higher-level comprehension. [14]

The negative effects on reading are emphasized by The Reading Research Quarterly. A review article on the effects of TV concluded that television:

- displaces leisure reading and thus inhibit the growth of reading skills.
- requires less mental effort than reading
- may shorten the time children are willing to spend on finding an answer to intellectual problems they are set to solve.
- has particularly negative effects for heavy viewers, socially advantaged children, an intelligent children." [15]

TV AND MEDIA TEACH VALUES

While TV has many effects on the brain, its ultimate effect is on its ability to teach values. What is modeled through television is processed and imitated by our kids. This becomes particularly important to Christian parents that are trying to prevent the conflicting values from taking root during the most formative years. The way that TV teaches is subtle. The largest bulk of teaching is not from the programming format of shows like Sesame Street. Rather, it is through imitation.

IMITATION

One of the strongest teachers of our children is imitation. The video *Plugged In* produced by the National Institute on Media and the Family contains an excerpt from a news story by Rick Kupchella (a TV Reporter here in the Twin Cities). In this expository story, he monitors children in a daycare center on two separate days behind two-way glass. The first day the toddlers watch *Barney*. Their play afterward is quiet and cooperative. The next day they watch *Power Rangers* and much to the surprise of everyone, their subsequent play is kicking and punching. Even the more shy and reticent children participated in the more aggressive play. This was after twenty minutes of viewing a TV show. [16]

As parents we need to be humbly aware that our children watch and imitate **us** in an even more powerful way. Who we are as children of God makes such a huge difference as it shines through to our children. There has never been a more convincing reason to walk an authentic Christian walk than realizing how potent imitation is as a teacher.

We are all teachers as parents. James 3:1 admonishes us that, "Not many of you should presume to be teachers, my brothers, because you know that we who teach will be judged more strictly." Parents are all teachers.

In everything set them an example by doing what is good. In your teaching show integrity, seriousness and soundness of speech that cannot be condemned, so that those who oppose you may be ashamed because they have nothing bad to say about us. Titus 2:7-8

Beth Moore writes, "God's teacher is the vessel while God's word packs the punch." [17]

What do our children observe at home? Can our children see God in the way we live? Do our children see us read the Bible? Do we pray together with our children? Can our children see our faith in action? How do our children see us interact with our world? Do we reach out to the hurting with love? Do we take our children with us to volunteer in areas where people are less fortunate or in need of help? Can our children see the mind of Christ in our actions?

What are they learning to imitate in terms of money management? How do we handle disappointments? How do we handle anger? The family is one of the only places they can learn healthy responses to anger in our media saturated world.

Can they feel love in the family? Are we building those relationships? Are we taking the time needed to build real relationships? They are worth our time. Do our children know they are valued? Frequently, children equate their value directly with the time we are willing to spend with them.

Although we will focus much of our attention in this book on what we actually teach our children with words, it cannot be emphasized strongly enough that imitation is the real key. We need to pay critical attention to our own personal walk with Jesus Christ. Let Him build us into the parents and role models we need to be for our children.

Find encouragement for your calling as parents in Ephesians 4:1-2 "As a prisoner of the Lord, then, I urge you to live a life worthy of the calling you have received. Be completely humble and gentle; be patient, bearing with one another in love."

One of my most vivid memories of motherhood was the day I realized the power of imitation in our home. It occurred at my youngest son's first grade parent-teacher conference. His teacher had saved a paper for me that Matt had written titled "All About Jesus." In it he was supposed to write as much as he could about Jesus. Matthew was 7. Nestled into the middle of the paper were the words 'my mom loves Jesus.' I am quite sure I never used the words "I love Jesus" in our home. Matthew picked it up in a way that startled me. He knew this relationship I have with our Lord Jesus Christ was something real. I will never forget my naïve level of surprise that Matthew had noticed. So, I wiped my tears and tried to listen to the rest of our conference; but, I don't think I heard another word his teacher said.

TEACHING DISCERNMENT

Teaching discernment starts when our children are young, and they learn there is a God and He is the creator of all life. They start to have a sense that the world follows the laws based on the character of its creator. It starts through the imitation we discussed. They watch what we do in the world. They pay attention to the direction we provide them with in terms of right and wrong in response to their behavior. These are the neural networks we lay down as a strong consistent foundation that our children will use when the prefrontal cortex starts its rapid development. It is essential when children are young that we teach their little brains what they should do. Try to avoid teaching with "No! No! No!" and "Don't do that!" Lay down the neural network that you want to replace the offensive behavior. Teach them what they should do!

However, when the prefrontal cortex starts to develop

a more challenging process of teaching discernment occurs. Now their brains will be able to complete tasks of abstract reasoning. This concept of right from wrong becomes a key focus in their development. Remember the research we showed by Harry Chugani? The young teen's prefrontal cortex is still different than your adult brain. It is in the process of laying down a tremendous number of neural connections during this age. They do not yet have an adult brain even though they are bigger than you are!

During these critical years, the first key to teaching discernment is to listen to our children. What did they hear us say? How did they process it? We need to talk less and listen more. We have to try to understand their thought processes. Remember, the prefrontal cortex is trying to pull together a lot of information we have helped them learn at a younger age. Now we need to help refine the process. This is where we need to challenge their neural circuits and strengthen their understanding.

> In the process of moral decision-making there is first the process of deciding what is right and wrong. Then there is the subsequent process of doing it.

These are two very separate processes in the young teen where peer pressure becomes so powerful. We have to know what is in their heart and what their 'process' is before we can shepherd them. We need to listen to our children. Simply watching what they do is not complete in the information it affords us! They may understand the process of making the correct moral decision but lack the fortitude to stand separate from their peers. We need to stimulate our children with questions at this age.

There are many great games for families to play that start the process of thinking through some of life's ethical dilemmas. Many are listed in the resources at the end of this book. The process of moral decision-making requires that our children make connections from many parts of the brain. It is helpful to bring that process into critical thought. We can help them understand the process of discussing the pros and cons to issues. We can help them start recognizing the consequences to decisions and build neural pathways that have God's Truth as their solid foundations.

Use care to manage anger appropriately in those teen years. Anger can become a big part of our relationships and interactions. Remember we are building neural pathways. We are the ones that need to train our child to develop healthy neural connections in their response to their anger. This training will bless them and their world for a lifetime. They have to be encouraged to make a stand and make a decision. Sometimes this involves conflict. Please remember that the rules of neural development are the same here in the prefrontal cortex as in other parts of earlier brain formation. The process can't be passive!

Proverbs 22:6 says, "Train a child in the way he should go and when he is old he will not turn from it." Train up a child in the way he should go and those neural pathways will be there to support your child throughout their lifetime of moral decision making.

Train a child in the way he should go and when he is old he will not turn from it.

Proverbs 22:6

Josh McDowell is a strong resource in the area of teaching our children right from wrong. In his book *Right From Wrong* he explains:

> If an objective standard of truth and morality exists, it cannot be the product of the human mind (or it will not be objective); it must be the product of another Mind. If a constant and unchanging truth exists, it must reach beyond human timelines (or it would not be constant); it must be eternal. If a universal rule of right and wrong exists, it must transcend individual experience (or it will not be universal); it must be above us all. Yet, absolute truth must be something – or someone - that is common to all humanity, to all creation. [18]

We live in a culture that is currently based in relativism. So, be prepared for the fact that your children will confront you and question your values. Are you prepared for the day that your child confronts you with the retort, "I just don't share your values!" Josh McDowell offers this as a way to explain absolute truth to our children. He says, "It's not what I know, nor what you know, that makes a thing wrong; **it's what God is** that makes it wrong." (Emphasis added) [19]

It's important to remind our children that we are not making up the rules. Rather, God trusts us to train them and shepherd their hearts along the precepts He has quite specifically laid out for us. Interestingly, current brain research shows that the developing mind perfectly follows God's rules.

"Too often, parents and other adults communicate to young people that their actions violate the adult's standard of decency, or ethics; or morality. That would be perfectly appropriate if absolute truth were defined by the individual. But it's not. It is God and God alone who determines absolute truth. Truth is objective because God is above all; it is constant because God is eternal. Absolute truth is absolute because it originates from the original." [20]

Remember that we need to help train the frontal lobes to make its associations. This part of the brain does not receive sensory input directly. All the information that gets laid down in neural networks in this area has to come from the connections the child made in earlier years.

We can help our children to understand the reasons behind what we are teaching them. We can provide them with the Truth and real reasons behind what is expected in their behavior. We can help them understand WHY they need to know something. We can help them see HOW it will affect them and other people. We can help them learn WHERE they can find guidance in God's Word.

Josh McDowell, in *Right From Wrong* shows parents how they can know truth. Websters Dictionary defines Truth as "agreement with a standard or original." [21] Can our children believe that God is the creator and originator of life? If they have no reason to believe this, it may be quite difficult to teach the existence of absolute truth.

Since God is the creator (the originator), all of his creation must follow His precepts and agree with Him. Truth in this world has to agree with the character of the maker. Truth has to agree with God, who is the original.

In medicine there are many examples of God's law being designed into the body. The body perfectly follows His precepts. For example, research on the origin of empathy actually shows that the cells in the brain for empathetic response are there at birth! [22] A newborn baby will trigger only certain cells of the brain in response to a sad crying face. We then, as parents, have to build on this pathway and strengthen it. Dr. Leslie Brothers in, *A Biological Perspective on Empathy*, writes;

> It is reasonable to assume that the capacity for empathy is present in some precursor form at birth in the normal brain and is elaborated by cognitive maturation and by subsequent experiences in the social milieu. [23]

In the processing of social signals such as facial expressions the data suggests;

> Even more recently, in the first systemic study using facial expressions as stimuli, Hasselmo et.al. (70) showed that a substantial fraction of face-selective neurons in the anterior superior temporal sulcus showed significant responses to expression. [24]

Does it surprise you that God designed cells in the brain to respond to facial expressions at birth? He designed empathy into us! He is love! As His creation we follow who He is!

The immune system is another wonderful example of God's law being designed into the body. We find repeatedly in science that the immune system components decrease in response to stress. That means that the body becomes susceptible to illness with high levels of stress. And some key areas of brain cells die off in a process called excito-toxicity as a response to stress. Christian parents can take heart because the information we know about how the body works completely supports God's law.

He asks us to trust Him and not give way to worry. He instructs us not to give way to anger. Worry and anger are two sources of stress to the human person. He asks us to walk alongside the needy and wounded and provide physical and emotional support to them. This lowers their stress and our stress! And, the growing literature that shows very high stress levels, sustained over time, leads to suppression of our immune system and then cell death is in the Bible as well.

- Proverbs 8:36 "But whoever fails to find me harms himself; all who hate me love death."

- Proverbs 11:19 “The truly righteous man attains life, but he who pursues evil goes to his death.”
- Proverbs 14:12 “There is a way that seems right to a man, but in the end it leads to death.”
- Romans 8:13 “For if you live according to the sinful nature, you will die; but if by the Spirit you put to death the misdeeds of the body, you will live.”

CHAPTER 5

MUSIC

Before we leave this discussion on the effects of media let's try briefly to discuss music. Music has a tremendous power in the human mind! It shapes our emotions! The relationship of music to brain development is absolutely fascinating. Most surprisingly, we do not learn to appreciate music. It is pre-programmed into our brains! And, not only can we recognize notes and tones and pitch, but we can recognize whole "contours" of music. [1]

"For example, we instantly recognize melodies as the same regardless of whether they are played by instruments that differ in pitch, or are played by the same instrument in a different key. Melodies are characterized by the exact intervals between pitches but even here, adults also pay attention to the pattern of increases and decreases of pitch, the so-called "contour" of a melody." [2] Sandra Trehub at the University of Toronto found that "infants 8-11 months of age do perceive and remember melodic contour." They recognize changes as little as one note! [3]

Dr. Weinberger cites another particularly interesting

study from T. Taniguchi of Kyoto University. In this study they "studied the accuracy of memory for words, according to the type of music present (2). He played either happy or sad music while subjects in different groups studied words that referred to personality traits either in a positive or negative manner. When tested later for word memory, performance was strongly affected by the type of music present. Positive words were better remembered if heard during happy music, while recall was better for negative words that were heard during sad music. Thus, congruency between music-induced mood and the affective meaning of language enhances memory compared to incongruency. So what we remember can depend on background music." [4]

It is important for us to recognize the impact of music when our children are young because music can facilitate learning. Hurwitz, Wolff, Bortnick and Kakas did the classic study in this area of learning in 1975. They used Kodaly training with folk songs, rhythm and melody to screen for effects on learning. "After training the music group exhibited significantly higher reading scores than did the control group, scoring in the 88th percentile vs. the 72nd percentile." [5] Music, it seems, helps the brain to make the connection between the sound of the word and visual part of the word. [6]

My passion to teach parents about music comes from watching the impact it has on our children when the cortex takes its leap in development around adolescence.

Music becomes a huge part of the lives of most adolescents and, therefore, most parents with adolescents. As secular lyrics are becoming more filled with anger and hate, parents are taking serious notice. At the same time, Contemporary Christian artists such as P.O.D. are trying to bring Christian lyrics into this aggressive musical genre. That, therefore, means they sing of

Christ's redeeming love within a musical style that is filled with anger. Isn't this against what Christianity stands for? Does it devalue the Word of God to sing it within music that speaks aggression, anger and hate to the emotional part of the brain?

Recognizing that we are designed to recognize contours of music, we must then recognize God as the designer. What type of music glorifies God and is consistent with his design? Frank Garlock and Kurt Woetzel say it this way:

> We must understand that man did not originate this miracle. He simply discovered the characteristics of sound behavior. And this small example allows us to see that God is not only the originator of music: He Himself is musical. He "sings" and "blows the trumpet," demonstrating that music is a part of His divine eternal being. Our music has developed from the attributes which He has created in sound here on earth." [7]

Kimberly Smith in her book *Oh, Be Careful Little Ears* tries to help make this distinction between what is God designed (spiritual) and what is carnal. She states, "carnal music...is music which appeals to our flesh through unnatural (improper) rhythms and/or other sensual devices. It may or may not contain lyrics. Spiritual music ("pure" music with a straightforward melody and no additional obtrusive rhythms or other sensual techniques) appeals to our spirit and glorifies God." [8]

I had never given this concept much thought until contemporary music became so vile. What does God intend for this gift of music? There is tremendous power in music. Do we consider any of this before allowing our children to listen to music? Many of us have been lulled to sleep and our ears can no longer discern what is Godly music. Majesty Music offers a videotape series addressing the pure nature of music and what makes it spiritual. [9]

Kimberly Smith advances her argument when she explains: "The reason this is not so clear to some is that their spiritual awareness of the sensuality in the music has been deadened in this area, simply by having experienced the stimuli (carnal rhythms, etc.) so often that they are no longer aware of how wrong the sensual response is. If we see, do, or hear something long enough, it becomes acceptable and no longer affects the conscience." [10]

The discussion of Contemporary Christian Music is quite complex. There are good resources at the end of the book if this is an area of concern for you. It is well worth more than a superficial glance if you have an adolescent at home.

Let's look again at groups like P.O.D. Focus on the Family's *Plugged In* interviewed Noah Bernardo the drummer for P.O.D. They explored some of these questions with Noah. He was well aware of the aggressive nature of their music, but then explained the love and passion for Jesus Christ of the band members. He explained that, "God determines where you grow up and what personality you bring to things. For everybody in the band, we came out of difficult situations, living a hardcore lifestyle before we knew Christ. Once we met Jesus, He took us as we were and let us write songs and perform them aggressively, but without the anger we grew up with. Instead, we've been driven by hard love that connects with certain music fans. But, keep in mind that this is all just camouflage. Playing is fun, but what we're all about is loving people and living for Jesus in a way they can relate to." [11]

The controversy that surrounds the use of God's Word in contemporary Christian music can divide a group of people with very little effort. There are also pro's and con's that can be supported by brain development information.

There is tremendous power in the way music affects the brain.

Let us make the basic assertion that MUSIC IS VERY, VERY POWERFUL. No, let's rephrase that. THERE IS TREMENDOUS POWER IN THE WAY MUSIC AFFECTS THE BRAIN. It's no mystery that music motivates us to move. It can change our moods and help boost spirits when we're discouraged. Music can keep soldiers marching when there is overwhelming monotony and fatigue. It can put a lift in chores when they are dull and routine. It makes the muscles practically move themselves with dance. It can also teach with the lyrics it carries. In fact, current research suggests that music may actually facilitate learning. It would be a safe bet that most of us remember many of the lyrics from the popular music when we were adolescents and teens. And, surprisingly, that would be true whether we were teens 10, 20, 30 or 40 years ago. Our Alzheimer-disease patients can frequently catch a glimpse of something familiar when they hear the songs of their very young childhood.

In his book, *The Closing of the American Mind*, Allan Bloom describes that, "Today, a very large proportion of young people between the ages of ten and twenty live for music. It is their passion; nothing else excites them as it does; they cannot take seriously anything alien to music." [12] This brings me back to Harry Chugani's PET scans. The brain is uniquely receptive to music during this time of development.

PET scans done by Dr. Michael Phelps and Dr. John Massioto show us what happens in the brain when we listen to music. As a person listens to music without lyrics the PET scan shows increased activity in the right hemisphere and the prefrontal lobes of the cortex. [13] The prefrontal cortex is our emotional part of the brain. Music is processed by the emotional part of the brain. The deep lasting effect of music comes from the way it affects us emotionally. And, although lyrics are also a factor, the emotional impact of the music will affect the neural networks to the greatest capacity. So, as in any form of media, the way music or its lyrics jolts our emotions will have the biggest impact on us.

Jane Healy explains:

> Brain studies have repeatedly shown that music, for everyone but highly trained musicians, is processed predominantly in the right hemisphere – in areas directly opposite those responsible for most language processing. Most of us listen and respond primarily in a holistic 'feeling' way to melody (right hemisphere's specialty), while musicians are trained to listen analytically to the technical sequence of notes and other features that must be handled by the left hemisphere. The relaxed state often induced by music is reflected in changes in brain-wave patterns: the more vigorous beta waves that characterize active mental processing yield to slower alpha waves, which are more commonly associated with relaxation. When parts of the brain are 'in alpha' they are essentially switched off from active thinking and learning." [14]

In any event, the search is underway to uncover how music affects the brain. One reviewer commented that "music therapy is known to have healing and relaxing effects. Although these effects appear to be mediated by release of neurotransmitters and neurohormones, the specific neurohormonal systems involved have not been fully investigated." [15]

There is some information about the response of the brain to music that we do understand. Here are some basics:

> "For example, "Meditative music has been found to decrease plasma cortisol and noradrenalin;" [in other words, it lowers stress], "prolactin decreased after modern music; classic music, on the contrary, did not affect the catecholamine system and HPA-axis function." (Mockel 1994) Remember, cortisol and noradrenalin (NE) are the chemicals high during stress. [16]

> "Techno- music [music generated by computers and electronic instruments] was associated with a significant increase in heart rate, systolic blood pressure and significant changes in self-rated emotional states. A significant increase was observed in B-endorphin, ACTH, NE, growth hormone, and cortisol after listening to techno-music. Classical music induced an improvement in emotional state, but no significant changes in hormonal concentrations." [17]

Can we actually understand the effects of contemporary music on the brains of our children? Dr. Jerre Levy remarked, "It's the nature of the music they're listening to, this popular music," she said. It is different from other kinds of music in that the tempo is exactly like a metronome: beat, beat, beat. Studies have shown that flashing lights at a fixed frequency (flash, flash, flash) sets up a rhythm in the brain that interferes with normal processing. The same may be true of the auditory system, she suggests." [18] Certainly if we look at the tumbling walls of Biblical Jericho we can see the effects of rhythmic beat on realigning molecules.

We know that classical music is about 60-100 beats/minute. Techno-music is 130-200 beats/ minute. Some researchers believe it is the tempo of the music with the frequency of beats that is what activates the chemical and hormone releases in the brain. [19] It may be the vibrations created by certain tempos or beats that results in the neurochemical release. This may in fact be true of the catecholamines in particular because they are manufactured and stored in the end-vesicles of the axon. [20]

One study states that, "These results support the findings of VanderArk and Ely (1992) demonstrating cortisol, norepinephrine and B-endorphin responses to music in general agreement with the evidence that fast music is able to activate the noradrenergic system and the HPA axis more than slow music." [21] Techno -music is the music of 'raves'.

Research studies, when they compared the classical to techno-music, found that , "Classical music induced an improvement of emotional state." [22] Techno-music, on the contrary, induced a worsening of the emotional state. There was a significant difference in the two types of music on the tense-relaxed scale, the anxious-calm, and the anguished-serene measurements. "During trial B, with techno-music, most of the subjects experienced tension, anxiety, a sense of 'urgency', trouble and anguish, while during the classical music they felt calm, serene and relaxed." [23] This music is increasing the release of the stress hormones! It is activating the fight or flight pathway!

Interestingly, when animals are in a quiet environment

but exposed to frequent discordant sounds they have difficulty learning. Animal studies with mice showed that animals raised in a quiet environment with arrhythmic drumbeats showed difficulty navigating a standard maze! [24]

Eric Jensen, in his book *Teaching with the Brain in Mind* sites that there is now persuasive evidence that our brain is already predesigned for music and the arts. [25] He describes a study in Aiken, South Carolina, where test scores were in the lowest 25% until a strong arts program was added and the percentiles soared to the top 5% in 6 years. He states, "This Title I rural school with a 42 percent minority student base showed that a strong arts curriculum is at the creative core of academic excellence – not more discipline, higher standards, or the three R's (Kearney 1996)." [26]

What is this incredible power in music? What is it doing in the minds of our kids? Jensen says that music does three things in the brain. First, it creates arousal in the brain. This means it either increases (peps us up) or decreases (relaxes us) the transmitters in the brain that create attention. This is what we just discussed above. It either excites the nerves or calms them down. Second, it is a carrier for words. The melody actually helps us learn the words. Thirdly, it is a primer for the brain. I think this is the key. Jensen describes, "There is a third, and quite powerful, use of music. It can actually prime the brain's neural pathways. Neurons are constantly firing. What distinguishes the 'neural chatter' from clear thinking is the speed, sequence, and strength of the connections. These variables constitute a pattern of firing that can be triggered or 'primed' by certain pieces of music." [27]

Ravi Zaccharias when describing the power of worship stated that "music gives structure to the emotions". He also warned that because of its power music can seduce as well as induce the emotions. [28]

This is what happens when anger builds on anger with the release of increased NE in heavy-metal and techno-music.

The auditory cortex does not just respond to sound frequencies but also to pitch and tones. Francis Rauscher says: “We know the neural firing patterns are basically the same for music appreciation and abstract reasoning.” [29] We tend to remember what is learned with music. Music “activates procedural (body) memory and therefore, is learning that lasts.” [30]

As we mentioned earlier, the brain is specialized for the building blocks of music. [31] The brain is made to recognize a ‘contour’ to music. This is similar to the lock and key pattern of molecular recognition seen everywhere in the body.

Look at the power of what this is saying! God has built into every human being a biological appreciation of music. This is a gift. God has designed music to be an awesome force.

So, with all this in mind, what about contemporary Christian music? The key to remember is that music initially will have an effect based on the neurochemicals already in balance in the child’s brain. In those children who have had chaotic violent lives they have high NE and cortisol levels as we will discuss in the section on anger. Remember, high NE is characterized by behavior that is over-aroused. It is ready for fight or flight. It therefore, has more impulsivity associated with it. One study noted that, “The preferences for heavy-metal and rap music seems to be in relationship to adolescent psychosocial turmoil: adolescents who prefer heavy-metal music had a higher incidence of below average school grades, school behavior problems, sexual activity, drug and alcohol use and arrests (Took and Weiss, 1994). [32]

We know certain things about Heavy metal fans from the sociology research that supports our suspicions that this musical genre is increasing the stress hormones and NE. Although the research done by Kevin Took and David Weiss focuses on psychosocial aspects of heavy metal music; it makes perfect sense from the brain physiology perspective as well. [33] As you look through this partial list of the characteristics of heavy metal fans, remember that high stress hormones make you more ready for flight or fight and, therefore, more impulsive. Nerves are more irritable and it takes much less stimulus to provoke anger. Frequently, it is a disrupted home that starts the cycle of high stress hormones in the brain.

The following data is found in *It's not Only Rock and Roll.*

- Heavy metal fans tend to be at odds with their parents and school environments and more closely allied with their peer group of other heavy metal fans.
- They are more likely than other youth to come from families in which the parents are either divorced or living separately.
- They express less satisfaction with their family than other youth.
- Relationships with parents either have open or smoldering conflict or when the relationships are satisfactory it is usually because the parents are permissive.
- They demonstrate less commitment to school, report more conflict with teachers and other school authorities.
- They perform less well academically. (Heavy metal is the only type of music that is consistently associated with decreased school performance.) [34]

When Norepinephrine levels are high there is also an associated reciprocal drop in serotonin and therefore, more depression. Consider this as we look at the final statistic regarding heavy metal music.

- Heavy use is associated with a vulnerability to suicide. (20% males/ 60% females reported deliberately trying to kill themselves in last 6 months compared to 8% male/ 14% female among general youth.) [35]

This response to music is highly individualized; just as the chemistry of their brain is completely unique to the individual. And reactions to music tend to be molded during brain development by what you are exposed to and the culture you are raised within. However, a constant diet of angry music will change the chemistry of the brain toward the higher stress hormones. We are beginning to see this behavior in the heavy metal syndrome making perfect sense.

North and Hargreaves tried to explain this further. "A simple summary of the North-Hargreaves study is that music seems to evoke emotions by doing two different things: (a) it produces a feeling of liking or disliking; (b) it produces a level of excitement or arousal. Neither of these two factors is itself sufficient to result in a particular emotion. But somehow they work together in the brain to yield actual emotions." [36]

With all this in mind, the ideal goal for parents is to encourage the music that will support the brain chemicals that lead to Godly behavior. This means we need to steer our children clear of the music that feeds anger and rage. Ephesians is very clear that we are to "Get rid of all bitterness, rage and anger, brawling and slander, along with every form of malice." Ephesians 4:31

So, it appears fairly straightforward that reinforcing anger in our children through the music that increases the anger neurochemicals like NE is warned against in the Bible. Music has a huge amount of power in our children because it can induce chemical changes in the brain. This can be a tremendous blessing in the way music can be used in healing. However, this is also the principle behind how strongholds form. If the brain of the child is like a flower, think of constantly increasing the stress chemicals through music as stepping on it.

So, as a goal for Christian parents, keep the anger-filled lyrics with the aggressive music genres out of the developing mind of your children.

Bad lyric + Aggressive genre= Don't Go There.

But, how do we make intelligent decisions about the good lyrics? What about groups like P.O.D.? As Eric Jensen notes above, music is also able to prime the neural pathways and make learning easier. Can it really bring a desire to seek Jesus Christ into a chaotic genre? Realistically, the high NE states that heavy metal music creates in the brain are designed for flight or fight; not contemplative learning. However, some learning of the lyrics will occur in this situation. And, it also seems to happen repeatedly, that God's people who have been wounded by the world have a special skill at reaching people with similar wounds. "Wuv" the drummer for P.O.D. understands the anger of that group of young people and he is drawn to bring the love of Jesus Christ into it.

Is it the best vehicle to carry God's message? No, because the music creates anger. Is it an acceptable vehicle to carry God's message into a culture that may not hear it any other way? Possibly. But, as the controversy rages, remember, it is relationships that will bring lost kids to Christ. Jesus Christ asks us to stand in the gap for Him as salt and light in the world. That's exactly what P.O.D. is trying to do inside a culture that few of us understand.

Kimberly Smith counters simply by stating: "This emotional high (or energy) that's experienced from carnal music actually inhibits us from seeking the true joy and freedom found in Jesus Christ. It's a cheap substitute for the energy that comes from being free from the power of sin. The energy that comes from being set free from the power of sin is from God." [37]

Please pray for the Holy Spirit to fill you with conviction and discernment regarding the use of music in the lives of your children.

One final note about music. The hearing part of the body is very sensitive to loud noise. NIH explains that hearing loss occurs at 85dB. Most rock concerts are 110-120 dB. [38] [39] [40] Our boys sat with their hands over their ears at the last Christian Concert we attended. We need to protect the hearing of our children. The small sensory cells of the cochlea do not repair themselves once they are injured. Repeated exposure to high decibel music destroys these cells. It knocks the sensory hairs down like they are trampled pieces of grass. Very quickly a beaten down grassy path becomes barren ground. Educate your children to protect their hearing.

CHAPTER 6

EMOTIONS AND ANGER

Emotions are universal. Eric Jensen describes that there are six common emotions across all cultures. These are "joy (pleasure), fear, surprise, disgust, anger, and sadness. Cross-cultural studies indicate that these six emotions are universal." [1] In this chapter our discussion will focus particular attention on anger.

Of all the human emotions, anger is one of the most potent and erosive. It is worthwhile taking extra time on this primary emotion from the perspective of its impact on parenting. Anger is a human emotion. That means that we will all experience it. Our children will experience it. It will try to consume us. But anger does not have to become sin. We can infuse our anger with evil based on what we decide to do with it.

As a primary principle for dealing with anger in our children, we need to remember that we are modeling to them the best ways to handle anger. The world is modeling to them violence as a way to solve problems on TV and in their video games. When you are defeated by anger in your parenting, please have the courage to apologize and point out a better way to your children.

Not only will this keep them aware of the spiritual battle that you struggle with as much as they do, but it will also remind them that they are incredibly valuable to you. You have no intention of wounding them. This lessens the possibility of those angry words becoming a deep part of their emotional person.

We are training the neural networks of our children. We need to find ways to teach them that control of anger is essential. Our children, as well as many of us, expect that we can tear apart another person with our anger and somehow a simple "I'm sorry" is supposed to heal all wounds. That is simply not true. Anger can be a tremendously potent toxin.

So, let's explore anger. The neurochemistry of this single emotion will amaze you! The thing about anger, versus other emotions, is that it tends to energize us. Angry music is energizing. Some of the most controversial secular music is sought after by our children who tell us they just 'like the beat.' This is probably true. Angry music is energizing; and it is speaking to the emotional part of the brain. One of the key reasons to talk about anger is that what we do with the environments of our children can not only affect whether they see the world as fearful or violent, but it can actually change the neurochemistry of the brain.

When it comes to anger, this is the key! Remember when we talked about Norepinephrine being one of our stress hormones? High Norepinephrine levels make us more impulsive and ready for flight or fight. This lowers the threshold for nerves to fire. This may well predispose us to anger (the shorter fuse). Research suggests that children who feel calm and secure with a parent have lower stress hormone levels. We buffer their stress. [2] We have a tremendous amount of power in the lives of our children.

Once Upon a Time

There was a father who instructed his young son to hammer a large nail into a piece of wood every time his son felt his anger was out of control. The son hammered many nails, for he was an angry boy. Gradually as time passed, the child learned to control his anger, and he hammered fewer nails into the wood. Finally, his father took him aside and commended him on how well he had learned to control his anger. The father then asked his son to remove the nails and bring him the wood. As his son complied, he noticed huge holes in the wood. Puzzled, he brought the fragmented wood to his father. His father took the wood and looked at him intently. Finally he said softly; "I want you to keep this wood to remember that each of those holes would have been a wound in someone's heart should you have chosen not to control your anger."

Paraphrased from a story by Tim Clinton Ed.D.
President, American Association of Christian Counselors [3]

Some of the newer information on the genes in the brain cells suggests that if the environments are consistently harsh for a child, the brain actually learns to modify the genes of the brain cells and create a permanent change in the brain.

Dr. Jeffrey Bland explains it this way: "The process that would have saved the life of the animal under acute stress now becomes the cause of shaping the phenotype for premature disease if it occurs over a long period of time as chronic stress." [4]

We are beginning to understand that early childhood parenting and the security of the home environment are very critical to the developing brain of the child. One recent study explains that;

> "The development of the brain is regulated by genes, that interact profoundly with early experience. The body's major biological stress systems, the hypothalamic-pituitary-adrenal (HPA) axis, and the catecholamine system (the locus ceruleus [LC] – norepinephrine [NE] / sympathetic nervous system [SNS]) are needed for survival. Overwhelming stress, such as child maltreatment experiences, may lead to alterations of these stress systems and adversely influence brain development."[5]

One of the ways that high stress triggers anger is by lowering the amount of stimulation that a nerve requires to fire. Constant high levels of stress hormones make the nerve more irritable. It gives us a short fuse. This can be the stress of child maltreatment, poor nutrition, hunger, dehydration, illness, and a complex array of psychosocial stressors. Even the constant bombardment from media and video games as they keep stimulating our attention center will release stress hormones. Remember, this attention center responds to stimulation by getting ready for flight or fight. It releases the stress hormones.

With the abundance of possible assaults on the development of our children it becomes essential that we train our children to think differently. Training them to keep God's truth at the core of their thinking will change this pattern of brain activity. Hopefully this will encourage a shift away from the upward spiral of stress hormones and away from the shorter fuse toward anger.

We discussed earlier the process whereby cells in the brain that are exposed to unrelenting high cortisol (our stress hormone) will eventually die off. It is a process that scientists call excito-toxicity. Nerves start to die in this high state of over-stimulation.

The nerve cells in the central amygdala send emotional messages out to the body. This area of the brain tells the blood pressure to go up and the heart to race. It controls the startle response and anticipatory fear. As these cells die off from continued stimulation these responses also die off. When this happens, the brain shifts from a high NE state to a lower NE state, and the emotional response dies off with that transition. Criminals become emotionless and cold-blooded. [6]

Painful, hard, stressful experiences increase NE and cortisol. Sometimes bad environments exist where there is emotional or verbal abuse. Sometimes it is physical or sexual abuse. Sometimes a bad environment is invited into our own living rooms through TV, video, computer and Internet. A high diet of violent programming can counteract weeks of Christian parenting. JAMA made an interesting statement in 1992: "It is concluded that the introduction of television in the 1950's caused a subsequent doubling of the homicide rate, i.e. long-term childhood exposure to television is a causal factor behind approximately one half of the homicides committed in the United States, or approximately 10,000 homicides annually. [7]

In your anger, do not sin. Do not let the sun go down while you are still angry, and do not give the devil a foothold.

Ephesians 4:26

ANGER BUILDS A STRONGHOLD OF SHAME

One of the strongholds that anger builds in us is shame. It reinforces shame in the person who is controlled by the anger, and it encourages the development of shame in the victim. When we lash out at our children in anger, they see themselves as fallible and not able to meet our standards. They will see themselves as the problem. They start to feel unworthy of our love, and the vicious cycle starts. This is the power that shame has in our lives and in our children.

GUILT IS DIFFERENT THAN SHAME

When we parent with God's Truth, we can guide children into the knowledge that a rule has been broken by their behavior. This is called guilt. It is quite different from shame. Parenting from this perspective encourages them to understand why we have that rule. God gives us rules for a reason. Remind them that there is a spiritual battle. Being tempted to break rules is to be expected when we are playing for such high stakes; but don't give up the fight! Keep striving to keep that relationship with Jesus Christ real. The battle is for their hearts. Let them know they are protecting their relationship with Jesus!

It is the highest thing in the world worth fighting for. Give them the NBA pep talk.

Here is a nugget to think about. TV commercials will reinforce the self-doubt of our children. Commercials feed them a constant diet of what they need to make themselves better. They operate from the premise that people are flawed and unworthy just as they are. Don't let TV and its constant diet of commercials keep shame alive in the hearts of your children.

When you are tempted to compare children with each other, remember that this is also a great way to build shame. Instead focus on the truth that God created each child unique and with special gifts. Katie might not be as good at spelling as Kim; but there is no reason she has to be.

Respond to their needs for comfort. It will buffer them from the storm as well as tame the beast of shame.

A gentle answer turns away wrath, but a harsh word stirs up anger. Proverbs 15:1

EMOTIONAL INTELLIGENCE

In 1990, Peter Salovy and John Mayer wrote a paper on Emotional Intelligence. They defined this term as "a set of skills hypothesized to contribute to the accurate appraisal and expression of emotion in oneself and in others, the effective regulation of emotion in self and others, and the use of feelings to motivate, plan and achieve in one's life." [8] This is an interesting concept because how we teach our children to deal with emotions sets them up for success or failure in life. It sets them up for health or disease. This is particularly true about anger.

Daniel Goleman in his book, *Emotional Intelligence,* defines it as:

1. Knowing one's emotions.
2. Managing emotions.
3. Motivating oneself.
4. Recognizing emotions in others.
5. Handling relationships. [9]

It is felt that much of the emotional intelligence of the human person is set in place in their first year of life. What we do with our anger becomes even more critical with this new concept in mind. We need to help our children build their ability to handle emotions in a truthful way and build healthy neural networks.

THE NEUROCHEMISTRY OF ANGER

Now let's try explaining the neurochemistry. Remember that emotions give our brain the signals to act. When the sympathetic nerves are firing, we feel fear and anger. These are our flight-or-fight signals. When the parasympathetic nerves are firing, we feel tender feelings and more calmness. All passion depends on the part of the brain called the amygdala. We are starting to recognize that it is the primary site of emotion in the brain.

One of the first myths that needs to be dispelled is that anger needs to be vented.

"Sometimes you just have to let it out," could not be farther from the truth. Daniel Goleman explains that when anger occurs, it releases NE as part of its initial flight or fight response, but then the amygdala does something very interesting. It stimulates the release of the stress hormones. Goleman calls this "a general tonic background of action readiness." [10] This new level of stress hormones can last for days and keeps the body in a state of readiness for any new threat.

> In general, the hair-trigger condition created by adrenocortical arousal explains why people are so much more prone to anger if they have already been provoked or slightly irritated by something else. [11]

Parents are often confused as to why children have a short fuse. Angry music builds anger. Angry TV programming builds anger. Research suggests that "overexposure to even nonviolent media can make kids more aggressive." [12] In the section on TV we discussed the stimulation to our alerting mechanism to keep our attention. The alerting mechanism is our "flight or fight" response. Once we are angry the brain sets us up with a shorter fuse for anger the next time because it has set us into readiness for a 'fight.' Eric Jensen explains:

> Early exposure to stress or violence also causes the brain to reorganize itself, increasing receptor sites for alertness chemicals.(Kotulak 1996). This increases reactivity and blood pressure and the child will be more impulsive and aggressive in school. [13]

We have a generation of angry children. How do we break the cycle?

What happens in the brain is that anger builds. If the next angry incident comes before the stress hormones are gone from the first one, they will intensify each other. As this starts a domino effect, it will intensify into rage.[14] Venting anger is not the way to stop the cycle. Giving way to anger only makes it worse. Goleman states, "Timing matters; the earlier in the anger cycle the more effective; indeed, anger can be completely short circuited if the mitigating information comes before anger is acted on" [15]

When you ask your teenager to cool off in his room, you are removing for them the environment where there will be more triggers for his anger. When you lower your voice while they are escalating; that removes potential triggers for more anger. God warned us that He placed this design for anger in the body.

Proverbs 22:24-25: "Do not make friends with a hot-tempered man, do not associate with one easily angered, or you may learn his ways and get yourself ensnared." If you want to really understand how God feels about anger and why He designed us this way do a topical search. My Bible has 36 references to anger.

H.A.L.T.!!!

This mnemonic is used to remind children of times that they are most vulnerable. Under these conditions the brain will be more irritable. Decisions will not be the best.

Hungry

Angry

Lonely

Tired

This mnemonic is helpful to children because stress from any source can increase our tendency to respond with anger. This is the whole point of the increases in stress hormones that create a shorter fuse. Tell children to **H.A.L.T**. and not to make any big decisions if they are Hungry, Angry, Lonely, or Tired. These tend to be some of the body's key stressors. Did you know that social isolation is one of the primary sources of increased stress? This is true for us as well as our children. They need us there. At a time when they are struggling to form an identity and have friends, we have to provide for them a safe haven of connectedness so that no matter how tough things are going with friends, they always have us!

One study on overt aggression showed the impact of this social connectedness. The authors concluded that: "These findings suggest that children's social adjustment may depend on the degree to which they obtain helpful, caring responses from peers, in addition to the degree to which they successfully avoid aggressive overtures." [16]

Try to become knowledgeable in child development. Learn what you can expect from a child at different ages. Remember the graph by Harry Chugani? The brain takes a long time to develop all the different parts. Sometimes a large part of the anger we direct at our children is the result of unrealistic expectations that we have as parents.

If you have a truly angry child, however, there are other resources available. Lou Priolo's book *The Heart of Anger* is very helpful to parents because it walks us through an examination of many of the potential causes for a child's anger. He describes a rebellion process that starts with a wounded spirit; which then germinates into bitterness. Bitterness shortens the fuse for anger. Anger practiced habitually becomes stubbornness. The process culminates in rebellion.[17].

Mr. Priolo explores with parents the way that we may be contributing to the development of anger in our children. Sometimes we are the ones who model sinful anger, or lash out in anger and call it discipline. Sometimes we are inconsistent in our parenting and our children truly do not understand what is expected. [18]

As parents we also need to put an end to the violent and anger-filled TV programs, video games, movies and music that are filling the minds of our children. These are lowering the threshold for anger. They are also teaching values

Lou Priolo reminds us of Colossians 3:21, "Fathers do not embitter your children, or they will become discouraged."

Many research studies are starting to point out the effects of this high level of anger on the body. *Circulation* in 1995 published an article showing that heart attacks could be caused by episodes of anger. This is a consequence of the high levels of stress hormones associated with anger. [19]

A meta-analysis (a large comparison of the research of many studies) done in 1987 of 229 studies of 'the disease prone personality' reports:

> Higher levels of anxiety, depression, anger, hostility, aggression, and extraversion are associated with a greater likelihood of heart disease. ....Regarding asthma, the variables of anxiety, depression, and anger/hostility/aggression are again positively and reliably associated with disease, but higher levels of introversion were reported with asthma. [20]

> Spouses of terminally ill patients experience a similar decline in various areas of immune function, including NK-cell toxicity, in the months following death of their partner. These same cellular changes have been noted in men and women during times of significant marital discord or following divorce. [21]

Do not be quickly provoked in your spirit,
for anger resides in the lap of fools.
Ecclesiastes 7:9

CHAPTER 7

FAMILIARITY and TEMPTATION

In the next chapters we will explore the spiritual part of our children. We will add the spiritual into our knowledge of the mind.

Let's preface everything we are going to discuss in this area of the spiritual battle with one unifying concept. That is, anything that is not God's TRUTH will be used by Satan to build strongholds. And, every aspect of the spiritual battle will be waged in the mind. He will use the lies of the world to tempt us and distract our focus off Christ. He will do it through the flesh with addictions that suck you dry rather than satisfy. He will do it himself as the great masquerader of truth in the form of an angel of light. This means our children will not recognize him unless they understand the character of God.

Our goal as parents will be to raise our children as spiritually discerning people. We need to help them understand the traps and learn to recognize the lies. It's a little like coming into your living room after a long family vacation and knowing something is different about that room. Before your vacation, your brain had visually recorded the contents of the room repeatedly, day after day. Suddenly, when it looks different (as in the TV disappearing) it sends you the alarm. Something is not right here.

Training our children is much the same, not quite so simple, process. They will consistently see God's truth in us and learn to "imitate", or recognize as familiar, spiritual wisdom and insight. When they are young they may only recognize when something is not as it should be. As they mature, they will recognize the spiritual attacks and know what they can use against them. They will be able to see and understand the bigger picture.

So, before we start feeling overwhelmed as parents in this task; let us claim 1 Corinthians 2:4-5 "My message and my preaching were not with wise and persuasive words, but with a demonstration of the Spirit's power, so that your faith might not rest on men's wisdom, but on God's power." We will fill their soda can with the experiences and teaching that will train them. Hopefully, they will accept and welcome the Holy Spirit's power.

Tony Evans uses a word picture of a National Basketball Association championship game. Encourage your children with this image that he creates. When the game gets tough you don't run to the sidelines and whine to your coach that the other players are blocking your shots. When you get the ball and the other team tries to knock it from your hands you don't give up. You recognize that you are the best-trained player on the court. With confidence you realize you have been trained by hours and hours of practice to anticipate the other team's moves and to neutralize them. [1]

Help your children feel confident that with the indwelling Holy Spirit they can handle what Satan flings at them. Help them feel confident in wearing their own spiritual armor and in accepting their own gifts and strengths. God will equip them to handle temptations. 1 Corinthians 10:12-13, "So, if you think you are standing firm, be careful that you don't fall! No temptation has seized you except that what is common to man. And God is faithful; he will not let you be tempted beyond what you can bear. But when you are tempted, he will also provide a way out so that you can stand up under it."

Be ready for the battle. In this current culture there is temptation everywhere. There is a lot at stake. Satan needs to tempt us to gain our permission to use our human person for his purposes. One of the reasons that our children do not recognize the battle is that it so common it becomes familiar. We live in times that the spiritual battle is everywhere and all the time. They are immersed in a youth culture that cannot discern the things that come from the Spirit of God.

"The man without the Spirit does not accept the things that come from the Spirit of God, for they are foolishness to him, and he cannot understand them, because they are spiritually discerned. The spiritual man makes judgments about all things, but he himself is not subject to any man's judgment: 'For who has known the mind of the Lord - that he may instruct him?' But we have the mind of Christ."

1 Corinthians 2: 14-16

FAMILIARITY

Let's talk for a brief moment about the flip side or the dual role that familiarity plays in the lives of Christian children. Remember in Mark 6:1-6 Jesus was not recognized in his hometown (those who were most familiar with him) as the Son of God. Jesus said, "Only in his hometown, among his relatives and in his own house is a prophet without honor." Mark 6:4. Remember the frog in the pot of boiling water? The longer he was in the pot, the more he grew desensitized and boiled to death. Beth Moore cautions us as Christians when she writes, "Casual familiarity is another weapon Satan uses against us in our fight to keep the faith. Sadly, some who've known Christ the longest have witnessed his power the least." [2]

Familiarity deadens us to the awe that we need to keep in our hearts regarding our spiritual heritage. It is a loss of the sense of wonder that we are created. It is a deadening to the amazing truth that our God is a personal God desiring intimacy with us. The more our children hear about their Christian roots without real evidence of a Christ relationship in us or developing in them; they will become desensitized to the greatest source of power in this world.

Ephesians 4:19 offers this warning about becoming desensitized to the battle and to our Power. "So I tell you this, and insist on it in the Lord, that you must no longer live as the Gentiles do, in the futility of their thinking. Having lost all sensitivity, they have given themselves over the sensuality so as to indulge in every kind of impurity, with a continual lust for more." Remember, we need to constantly bring meaning and understanding into our thinking to prevent this desensitization.

"Do not conform any longer to the pattern of this world, but be transformed by the renewing of your mind. Then you will be able to test and approve what God' s will is – his good, pleasing and perfect will."

Romans 12:2

From the brain development perspective, be ready for desensitization as parents. It is real. What the brain decides is 'unimportant'; it stops recognizing! That's OK. The brain has to limit the things it considers important or we would never accomplish anything. Just keep renewing the mind and telling it, 'this is important.' Renewing the mind is a part of what God intended by commanding us to 'Keep Holy the Sabbath Day.' It gives us one day of the week to focus on Him. It gives us a place in our week to let His spirit teach us and let our soul cry out with praise and thanksgiving. We need a time of quiet and peace for true renewal of the mind to happen. Renewing the mind is what we do when we begin and end our day in God's Word. It also puts breaks into our accumulating stress!

Inside the brain, the amygdala becomes **'desensitized.'** Our brain gets the signal that something is happening and then later decides it can lower its attention to that. The amygdala becomes less aware of the emotional significance of a threat or occurrence. Fabio Bordi did the research in this area using noise (sound) stimuli.

> Bordi was able to divide the acoustically stimulated cells into two classes; habituating and consistently responsive. Habituating cells eventually stopped responding to the repeated sound, suggesting that they might serve to detect any sound that was unusual or different. They could permit the amygdala to ignore a stimulus once it became familiar. ...The consistently responsive cells had high-intensity thresholds: only loud sounds could activate them. " [3]

This is the same reason that TV and movie producers need to keep raising the jolts to keep you watching their programs. Our brains turn off!

TEMPTATION

The only power Satan has is to tempt us! Always remember that he has already been defeated. His goal is to make sin look so attractive that we will replace Christ with a different idol on the throne of our heart. In the introduction, we talked about how only we ourselves can re-extend power to Satan who has already been defeated. Evil ultimately needs us to inject it with power!!

Temptations entice us. They draw us away from God by creating doubt that He is real, or creating confusion about the meaning of what God said, or creating so much discouragement we think God can't possibly do what He promised. James 1: 13-15 teaches us that, "When tempted, no one should say, 'God is tempting me.' For God cannot be tempted by evil, nor does he tempt anyone; but each one is tempted when, by his own evil desire, he is dragged away and enticed. Then after desire has conceived, it gives birth to sin; and sin, when it is full-grown, gives birth to death."

Interestingly, the current research on the immune system shows that stress (anger, worry, anxiety, bitterness, rage, loneliness) all suppress the immune system and lead to more illness and disease. As we discussed earlier, sustained levels of stress cause the dying off of cells in the brain. Reclaim Sunday as a day to keep a scheduled break in the stress. Use it to bring your family closer. Use it to draw closer to God.

Interesting new research suggests that one of the reasons that stress makes us feel so tired is that high stress hormones activate the gene for making rT3 and turn off T3 (active form of thyroid hormone). T3 when it combines with retinoic acid is responsible for the release of energy from our mitochondria. If there is lower T3; there is decreased energy that will be released from our mitochondria. [4] All of God's creation follows His laws. He has repeatedly asked us to trust Him rather than walking the road of stress.

Sometimes our tendency to reason things out and to be drawn away from Christ by persuasive arguments is a form of temptation. We start to rationalize that sin is OK. Martin Luther saw the trap of reason when he stated, "Reason is the greatest enemy that faith has: it never comes to the aid of spiritual things, but – more frequently than not - struggles against the divine Word, treating with contempt all that emanates from God." [5]

One of the most unfortunate aspects of temptation in our current culture is that we do not recognize it at all. Most of us, hopefully, know that we are struggling and we have internalized a strong sense of right from wrong. We frequently fail because this is a fallen world and we are not perfect. But we have a sense of the broken relationship with Christ Jesus. When I sin He let's me see the way my sin will work in the lives of my children. And, that breaks my heart. It makes me feel totally immobilized in my role in the Body of Christ. In other words, it distresses me.

Many of the children of this generation have no real sense of right and wrong. Everything is acceptable. "Whatever." They have learned to make their choices about right and wrong based on how things feel. They have learned to "trust their instincts." If it feels good; it must be alright. This is the current youth culture. Our children are part of it.

Ron Hutchcraft alerts us in these words: "Unfortunately, sin is a non-issue to today's children. Playing on a field where they see no boundaries, they feel no sin problem. And since sin is a non- issue, a savior is also a non-issue." [6]

Part of the anti-Christian sentiment that exists in our culture comes from the absolute lack of understanding as to why we need a savior. The Christian faith, as we mentioned above, seems like complete foolishness to them. To non-believers looking in, the Christian faith seems like a lot of rules. They don't understand that Jesus Christ is real. Everything is based on our relationship with Him. When we are distressed by temptation and sin, it is because it breaks this relationship we have grown to experience and cherish.

All of creation is based on those rules that appear as foolishness to those who have not yet met Jesus Christ. And breaking those rules violates what we understand to be the character and precepts of God.

CHAPTER 8

EMOTIONAL INTELLIGENCE and EMOTIONAL WOUNDING

Everything that is not God's Truth can be used to create pain, hurt, and suffering in this world. When I think of the capacity that this world has to wound the very core of a person's being, I think of the evil that is necessary to accomplish this. Unfortunately, many of us have been wounded. Sometimes those people that are closest to us unwittingly injure us with words and emotional abusiveness. Sometimes wounding is more direct, through physical abuse or sexual abuse. These emotional wounds frequently become a stumbling block for parents who are trying to establish healthy patterns of parenting.

For that reason, let's discuss this process of emotional wounding versus emotional intelligence. We mentioned earlier that the process of empathy is already in place when a child is born. The infant brain recognizes different expressions on the human face. In the first year of life, therefore, those cells in the brain are getting the signal from us about whether they should become stronger or weaker. The neural networks for the response to emotions get established.

Brent Curtis and John Eldredge in the *The Sacred Romance* describe this critical place in development this way:

"What does any of this have to do with our heart? God created each of us with a unique identity, a role in the larger story, but early on we've been handed a revision by the other players in our life." [1]

This introduces the concept of emotional intelligence and emotional wounding. God has a perfect plan for each of his children. If we are growing in an environment that nurtures the child we tend to develop more along with God's design. When the child is not nurtured that script tends to be rewritten. The end result is that God's plan is hindered by those closest to us.

Emotional wounding prevents us from seeing the true plan God has for us. Earnie Larsen teaches that "What you live with; you learn. What you learn; you practice. What you practice, you become. What you become has consequences." [2] Wounds become part of our thought process itself when we are repeatedly told or shown that we are not valuable or beautiful or worthwhile. Wounds become part of us when we live with parents who are unhealthy emotionally and their contribution toward the building of our of our neural networks leaves us feeling that we are not worth much in this world. We feel unloved. We definitely don't feel valuable. Please realize that nothing can be farther from the truth!!!

Do you see how **lies** (i.e. that you are not valuable), that are definitely not originating from God, wound us? This is not originating from God's truth. The confusion builds because these are lies told to us by the people who are our mirror in the world. When we are wounded we walk around filled with shame and a sense of unworthiness. And yet, the TRUTH is that our God pursues us persistently throughout our lifetime. He created us with such attentiveness and care! He loves us enough to come to earth and give us His Word in the physical form of Jesus Christ. And, He loves us enough to die a horrible humiliating death in order to accomplish that task. It was not His design for your script to be rewritten.

God has such an incredible plan for us. It is important to remember that while wounds are very real and painful; the person doing the wounding is usually playing with the best cards they have. Unfortunately, the skills and judgment they function with are sub-optimal and create much pain in the lives of those around them. But, frequently it is the only reality that our parents knew. They practiced patterns of parenting that came from their parents and the generations before them. Many of the parents who wound their children have been wounded themselves. This repeating cycle is one of the ways that the sins of a generation are passed down.

When God gave the ten commandments to Moses in Exodus 20:4-6 He said, "You shall not make for yourself an idol in the form of anything in heaven above or on the earth beneath or in the waters below. You shall not bow down to them or worship them; for I, the LORD your God, am a jealous God, punishing the children for the sin of their fathers to the third and fourth generation of those who hate me, but showing love to a thousand generations of those who love me and keep my commandments."

What is the idol in the heart of the one who wounds? Is it the satisfaction of the flesh though an addiction? Is it anger? Something is on the throne of their heart other than Jesus Christ.

You see, the wounds, hurts and pains of our parents were the lies they believed and passed down to us. The one thing I have learned, almost without exception, is that parents truly parent with the best cards they have. If they knew a better way, they would employ it.

One of my patients told me how betrayed she felt when her alcoholic mother actually looked at her with love in her eyes. After all the years of feeling unloved, she caught a glimmer of real love in her mother's eyes. Do you have the courage to let Jesus guide you into forgiveness and trust Him to break the pattern of wounding with this generation? Can you make the commitment to pass on a more truth-filled heritage to your children? His Word, as we will soon see, is living and real. His Word heals those wounds.

One of the reasons that it is hard for many of us to believe God's love is because those very people who many times did the wounding were also giving us a glimpse of God. Ironically, many times our parents provide us with our first views of a "Father God" through the love we receive through them. Chaotic, abusive and wounding environments also build a hyper-vigilance within the chemistry of ours brains. It becomes very difficult to trust and feel safe. We end up keeping God at arms length because we have no inner vision of real unconditional "Love."

Many times we need another caring, consistent person to come along side us in our life and just be there. We need that person to slowly and steadily let us trust them until we see unconditional love through them. You see, God doesn't abandon us when we are wounded. Rather, He continually prompts His people to be in the world as salt and light. He continually asks His people to be His hands in a world that is filled with hurt. He sends His people into the world to sit alongside the wounded to listen and love. He asks His people to live lives free of busyness so we can hear and recognize a heart that is crying out. He asks us to walk with the wounded and to let them meet Him and feel His love through us. We are the way Jesus works here on earth through His body of believers.

The miraculous, incredible, tremendous thing that happens next, is that as we heal from our inner wounds we become specially equipped for reaching out in love to people that have been wounded in the same way. As we experience the incredible power of healing that occurs in our life from and through Jesus Christ, we long to tell others that there is another way. We understand **exactly** what they are feeling. We don't necessarily understand the healing we received, but we are compelled toward people that are shackled under the tyranny of their wounds to let us introduce them to Jesus, the healer of all wounded souls. However, the authors of *The Sacred Romance* also explain that, "For some of us, that healing will come without the reconciliation with those who have harmed us. Nothing is impossible with God." [3]

Let's take a moment and look at why wounding happens. Most of the time wounding happens when we are children letting every word and action from the people we love program our young minds. And, as we discussed earlier in the research of Harry Chugani, our more discerning processing centers of the brain are not developed well enough yet to act as a buffer. Our brain records information deep in the emotional centers. We don't have the capacity in the brain until around age 8 to keep this information in perspective. We cannot recognize the lies. We don't understand that this was never God's plan. Then we struggle and wonder why in the world we make the decisions we do once we become adults. We are unaware of the power behind the lies we have grown to believe. They are part of us!

Children who have been raised with childhood sexual abuse, violence or physical abuse, develop neural networks in their brain much like Post-traumatic Stress Disorder (PTSD). A child learns to be constantly vigilant because there is usually no predictable pattern to when the abuse will occur. This process occurs in violent and abusive lives that are not buffered by the love and consistent care of a nurturing parent.

These children develop high levels of stress hormones and norepinephrine in their brains. Remember, norepinephrine is the flight or fight neurotransmitter. These children learn to be constantly ready to respond to a threat via sexual abuse, violence or physical abuse. Their environment does not allow them the luxury of letting their guard down. They are constantly vigilant, being 'on guard' to the possibility of another threatening event. The brain subsequently learns and grows in response to this constant supply of norepinephrine and stress hormones. High stress usually also means low serotonin. The low serotonin then creates feelings of depression. The cycle continues.

Children that develop high norepinephrine tend to startle and explode with anger more easily. Interestingly, even very high levels of stress during pregnancy can create a situation where the fetus develops higher than normal norepinephrine levels. Remember we discussed that high cortisol levels, which is our stress hormone, finally lead to the dying off of some of the brain cells? Very high stress also interrupts the process called Long Term Potentiation (LTP) in the hippocampus. This area is needed for explicit memory pathways to form. When it gets interrupted we don't remember well. This is what happens in the brain when we are wounded. Counselors call these "Repressed Memories."

The world we provide for our children gives them a safe environment to buffer the stress. Children need routines, consistency and familiarity. The unconditional love that we give to our children gives them a view of God and helps them to trust Him and their world. The way we live in our homes with our children gives them a perfect substrate to imitate. The time is now! There will never be a more compelling reason for us to reach out to Jesus Christ, sometimes through skilled counselors, to heal our inner wounds. Remember, our children are watching us live. They learn through imitation more effectively than anything else. Let us become the parents we long to be. Let us become the parents they will want to imitate.

It is time to reach out for healing if you are struggling

with childhood wounds. Let the wounding end with our generation! Bring a copy of this page to your pastor for help If you are struggling and don't know where to start. Ask him to help you or guide you to a skilled Christian counselor. Please claim the hope we have in Jesus Christ. His healing is real.

God keeps His promises. If you are wounded claim this promise: Joel 2:25 "I will repay you for the years the locusts have eaten."

Now, let us look at healing from the brain perspective. Our childhood wounds are imprinted in the area of the brain called the amygdala. This is the part of the limbic system that gives a strong fearful emotional response to things. It tells us what to avoid. It tells us what brings us pain rather than pleasure. Now, remember that we talked about this amygdala connection when we were talking about TV, because TV also talks to the emotional parts of the brain in children. The amygdala also connects to the prefrontal cortex, which is part of the thinking brain. It starts its rapid development in late childhood and early adolescence. This is how healing will eventually occur. Once this area of the brain forms and we are able to safely bring these memories and lies into the cortex they become less powerful. Once we can slowly bring them into conscious thought from that emotional center of the brain, then the beast can be given a name and can be exposed for the lies that created him. This is when the divine process of forgiveness, through God's incredible grace allows us to evict the beast forever. Don't ever lose sight of the TRUTH that you are incredibly loved and capable of being the parent you desire to be! God has a wealth of healing and wisdom ready for your hurting heart.

Emotional wounds are recorded into the amygdala as children. Healing from these wounds can occur when the brain matures, and the cortex finally develops. The development of the prefrontal cortex is key in the healing from emotional wounds. Researcher Maria Morgan has shown that "when part of the prefrontal cortex is damaged, emotional memory is very hard to extinguish." [4] Similarly, Davis found that blocking the NMDA receptors where the cortex sends its signals down to the amygdala "interferes with extinction. Those results hint that extinction is an active learning process." [5] Once we learn to feel safe with another human being and start to bring those memories into consciousness; they can be exposed for the lies that built them. Extinguishing these memories is an active process. It is a process that requires the healing grace of Jesus Christ.

Emotional Intelligence

As we discussed earlier emotional intelligence is "a set of skills hypothesized to contribute to the accurate appraisal and expression of emotion in oneself and in others, the effective regulation of emotion in self and others, and the use of feelings to motivate, plan and achieve in one's life." [6]

In other words, how we respond to the hurts and sadness of our children will build emotional intelligence. This is the basis of the Christian home! If we as parents are able to cling to Jesus Christ as our source of power and wisdom, our children will feel that love. The result will be children that are emotionally intelligent rather than emotionally wounded. The result will be children that will be able to recognize God's script for their life. Help your children to develop the ability to handle emotions in a truthful way. Help them build healthy neural networks. Keep their focus on The One who makes the rules and writes the scripts!

CHAPTER 9

STRONGHOLDS

While we're talking about the spiritual part of children let's look at how strongholds develop in the mind. This is particularly important for us to understand as parents so we can sabotage the strongholds we see our children developing and reroute those pathways toward more truthful thinking. Remember our premise? Everything that is not God's TRUTH will be used by Satan. A spiritual stronghold is anything that is a lie that we believe. Once we believe it we make it part of the permanent structure of our brain by playing it over and over again to ourselves. This is a key point! The thought processes we use the most often will become the dominant neural networks that are most deeply molded into the brain. This is especially true of the thought processes we establish into our neural networks as children.

In the human person we are divinely created to have God fit perfectly in the center of our thoughts. Every part of the human body is made up of receptors and perfectly fitting molecules that fit that receptor.

Ravi Zacharias says, "The old adage still speaks: The world was made for the body, the body was made for the soul, and the soul was made for God." [1]

Our soul is perfectly designed for Him! We are designed for Him to fit at the center of things. Our bodies also work according to His divine plan. Remember, He is TRUTH. So, one way to look at strongholds is to think of them as any thoughts that are allowed to develop that are lies (not the TRUTH) that will set us up in opposition to allowing God or Jesus Christ reign at the center of our mind. Paul explains this concept of strongholds in 2Corinthians 10:5 when he says, "We demolish arguments and every pretension that sets itself up against the knowledge of God, and we take captive every thought to make it obedient to Christ." The NKJV calls strongholds, "every high thing that exalts itself against the knowledge of God."
(2 Corinthians 10:5).

Beth Moore, in her book on *Breaking Free from Spiritual Strongholds*, describes this process like this. She says;

> A stronghold is anything that exalts itself in our minds, 'pretending' to be bigger or more powerful than our God. It steals much of our focus and causes us to feel overpowered. Controlled. Mastered. Whether the stronghold is an addiction, unforgiveness toward a person who has hurt us, or despair over a loss, it is something that consumes so much of our emotional and mental energy that abundant life is strangled – our callings remain largely unfulfilled and our believing lives are virtually ineffective. Needless to say, these are the enemy's precise goals. [2]

So, in this spiritual battle for the mind, it will really help us if we can understand the world, the flesh, and the devil in practical terms. We have to be able to know the enemy and how war will be waged against us and against our children. Next, we have to fully accept the fact that this war is a spiritual battle. We have been given specific weapons for war. We need to understand our spiritual armor in a very practical way. If **we** don't understand the process, we cannot adequately equip our children.

And, remember the child wrapped in bubble-wrap? That is only effective until we can dress them in their spiritual armor. It is only effective until we can nurture their understanding of the value and role of that armor in their life.

2 Corinthians 10:3-4 says, "For though we live in the world, we do not wage war as the world does. The weapons we fight with are not the weapons of the world. On the contrary, they have divine power to demolish strongholds."

The World

The world can be viewed as all the things that man has created. This might include things like the social structure and our climb for social status. Jobs are part of the world. Money and all the 'things' it can buy are part of the world. The world is all the distractions that provide diversion and excitement. The world is the interrelationships of people, our neighborhoods, the pecking order and the pyramid of success.

When the world takes our focus away from Jesus Christ we usually put man on the throne in His place. We care more what men think about us than what God thinks. We desire to be known for our possessions and our accomplishments. We place the roles we play in the world above our divine purpose. The opinions and the esteem of men replace God on the throne. We care strongly about what people think and say about us.

We care a lot more about the things of men than the

things of God. We strive more for the things we can accomplish and accumulate in the eyes of men than asking God to use our hands for His work. The trappings of the world are immense because this is our every day culture. It is what we live and experience day to day with our five senses. And, especially as infants and children we grow and thrive based of the love and relationships we have in that physical world. We condition ourselves in a certain way to do and act in ways that will bring the kinds of love we desire into our lives. But, this is the key! **As long as we feel we have to earn love, the world remains a big player in our strongholds.**

Three key verses to study in trying to understand the workings of the world are:

Romans 12: 2-6 "Do not conform any longer to the pattern of this world, but be transformed by the renewing of your mind...For by the grace given me I say to every one of you: Do not think of yourself more highly than you ought, but rather think of yourself with sober judgment, in accordance with the measure of faith God has given you. Just as each of us has one body with may members, and these members do not all have the same function, so in Christ we who are many form one body, and each member belongs to all the others. We have different gifts according to the grace given us."

1 John 2:15-17 "Do not love the world or anything in the world. If anyone loves the world, the love of the Father is not in him. For everything of the world- the cravings of the sinful man, the lust of his eyes and the boasting of what he has and does- comes not from the Father but from the world. The world and its desires pass away, but the man who does the will of God lives forever."

James 4:4-6 "You adulterous people, don't you know that friendship with the world is hatred toward God? Anyone who chooses to be a friend of the world becomes an enemy of God. Or do you think Scripture says without reason that the spirit he caused to live in us envies intensely? But he gives more grace. That is why Scripture says 'God opposes the proud but gives grace to the humble.' "

The Flesh

The flesh, on the other hand, is made up of all the desires and urges that come as part of our human body. Fleshly temptations are the ones that will bring pleasure to the body. We cannot discipline the flesh to go away. The fact that certain things bring us pleasure is part of being human. However, we can train our responses to the flesh.

When our strongholds rest in our flesh we are on the throne. Our desire to satisfy our self becomes central to our thoughts and God is preempted from His rightful throne. We decide that our comfort and desires are more important than what God is asking to do with us here on the earth. The interesting thing about the brain circuits that satisfy the flesh is that they are never satisfied!

Addictions establish themselves in the brain and actually change the brain chemistry! We'll discuss this in the section on Internet pornography. And, the neuro-transmitters that are released as the response to pleasure create a feedback loop that makes us want more. Very quickly what used to satisfy, is no longer enough and we seek more. Our flesh holds us hostage. Ephesians 4:19 explains that once we give ourselves over to sensuality there will be a continual lust for more. That is exactly what happens in the brain. God establishes the laws for how the body will work!

Find encouragement in Paul's words when he says, "It is for freedom that Christ has set us free. Stand firm, then, and do not let yourselves be burdened again by a yoke of slavery." Galatians 5:1. Our yoke of slavery is this process of addiction that the flesh sets up in our mind. Self-indulgence desensitizes us to the messages from the Holy Spirit. When I am insatiable in the way I choose to feed my flesh, I will seek more satisfaction from the flesh. The brain starts seeking that which gives it pleasure. The cycle goes on and on.

Satan will use our flesh to build strongholds. There are tremendous temptations in the world to tempt the flesh of our children. Once these strongholds develop they seem to create a never-ending internal battle for the wholeness of our souls.

1 Peter 5:8-9 says, "Be self-controlled and alert. Your enemy the devil prowls around like a roaring lion looking for someone to devour. Resist him, standing firm in the faith, because you know that your brothers throughout the world are undergoing the same kind of sufferings."

Teaching our children to have control of 'the self' is essential. The normal cravings of our body have to be understood and placed in a truthful perspective. Proverbs 25:28 "Like a city whose walls are broken down is a man who lacks self-control."

The temptations of the flesh are very similar in Colossians 3, Galatians 5, Matthew 15 and Mark 7. Galatians 5:19 lists them as "sexual immorality, impurity and debauchery; idolatry and witchcraft; hatred, discord, jealousy, fits of rage, selfish ambition, dissensions, factions and envy; drunkenness, orgies, and the like."

Matthew 15:19 says, "For out of the heart come evil thoughts, murder, adultery, sexual immorality, theft, false testimony, slander." Remember, these sins are common to all of us.

Pride is one of the most difficult sins to recognize because it is our own self-talk. And, it is especially hard to monitor in the developing child because they are in the process of acquiring skills and learning to feel confident in their own abilities. Pride becomes a stronghold when we see our own personal 'self' as more important than the big picture. We have to develop skills and talents and wisdom to be effective in the world. But, we have to keep an eternal perspective on where those talents came from. We have to encourage our children to maintain their innocence and humility while, at the same time dispelling their naiveté regarding the traps of the world and the flesh. In Matthew 10:16 Jesus said, "I am sending you out like sheep among wolves. Therefore, be as shrewd as snakes and as innocent as doves."

Deut. 8:17-18. "You may say to yourself, 'My power and the strength of my hands have produced this wealth for me.' But remember the Lord your God, for it is he who gives you the ability to produce wealth."

The final two areas of the flesh we will discuss are the strongholds of busyness and fear. These are two huge areas for parents and children alike.

BUSYNESS

Busyness is probably the most common trap of all for parents. It never goes away without conscious daily effort to control and maintain it! Busyness puts a lot of non-essential things on the throne instead of Christ. Many times they are the nonessentials we wish, as parents, weren't there anyway. Busyness steals our time. It steals our time away from Jesus. We need this time every day to renew our minds and gain wisdom and insight into our current parenting issues. We need this time so Jesus Christ stays a familiar friend and every day is welcomed to sit on the throne of our hearts. It steals teaching time away from our children. We have a lot to accomplish as parents in equipping our children and keeping God's laws familiar to them.

We need time together with our children to strengthen the trust and the consistency that will underlie our relationships with them. Time is so valuable as a parent. Don't surrender it to the nonessential. Reread Luke 10: 38-42 and focus on what the Holy Spirit is trying to say to you about busyness.

> "But Martha was distracted by all the preparations that had to be made. She came to him and asked, 'Lord, don't you care that my sister has left me to do the work by myself? Tell her to help me!' "Martha! Martha!' the Lord answered, you are worried and upset about many things, but only one thing is needed. Mary has chosen what is better, and it will not be taken from her." Luke10:40-42.

FEAR

Let's start our discussion of fear with 2 Timothy 1:7 "God has not given us a spirit of fear, but of power and of love and of a sound mind." When Satan works on us in the areas of our fears he convinces us that we are alone and we can't handle the situation at hand. We are talked out of believing that God will do what He says He will. The power of His Spirit is still there. In fact, his power is even greater when we are weak and not walking through life on our successes. We need to ask the Holy Spirit to enable us to do what we need to do in fearful situations. We become too fearful to believe God. What would happen if we really trusted him? What if we fell flat on our face? What if we appeared foolish? What if we miss out on good things in life?

Fear weakens our hold on the shield of faith. Beth Moore explains that, "To increase our vulnerability to a full fledged attack, Satan hesitates at nothing to create an atmosphere where fear abounds. He takes advantage of our fear of disappointment, our fear that

God might not 'prove' His love to us, and our fear of humiliation before others." [3] In the Bible some incredible faith was displayed in fear-filled times. Hebrews 11:23 "By faith Moses' parents hid him for three months after He was born, because they saw he was no ordinary child, and they were not afraid of the king's edict."

Hebrews 11: 27 "By faith he left Egypt, not fearing the king's anger; he persevered because he saw him who is invisible."

An interesting aside from the brain development information is that violence in our society increases fear. We have become increasingly fearful as a culture as the amount of violent programming has increased in the past twenty years. Many great sins are born from fear. When fear is allowed to exist and take hold, faith will begin to wither. Ezekiel 28 explains the beginnings of Satan. Verse 16 states, "Through your widespread trade you were filled with violence, and you sinned." It's interesting to see how Satan with his hand for violence in our world works through fear in the general culture to knock the shield of faith away! Revelation says of Satan, "But woe to the earth and the sea, because the devil has gone down to you! He is filled with fury because he knows that his time is short." Rev. 12:12.

SATAN

This then brings us finally to a discussion of Satan. He is real. When Jesus sent out the twelve He gave them very simple instruction about the evil forces in the world.

> Matthew 10: 26-28, "So do not be afraid of them. There is nothing concealed that will not be disclosed, or hidden that will not be made known. What I tell you in the dark, speak in the daylight; what is whispered in your ear, proclaim from the roofs. Do not be afraid of

> those who kill the body but cannot kill the soul. Rather, be afraid of the One who can destroy both soul and body in hell."

We need to fear God, not Satan. Remember, he has already been defeated. Teach your children not to let him defeat them.

There are certain predictable ways that he operates. We've talked about how he builds fear. He loves to work in us through pride. He constantly wants us to test God's promises and he challenges the relevance of God's Word in our lives today. Sometimes he gains our worship through hate filled music. We only get glimpses of the war that Satan rages against God. But, predictably he will attack any gift from God intended for us as His beloved! He will attack our peace and joy with fear. He will attack the gift of sexuality with perversion as well as 'desensitization' so we no longer recognize the beauty and transcendence of the gift. He attacks the beauty and gift of life with his violence and death.

James 4:7-8 advises us to "Submit yourselves, then, to God. Resist the devil and he will flee from you. Come near to God and he will come near to you."

1 Peter 5:8 "Your enemy the devil prowls around like a roaring lion looking for someone to devour." Satan only has the power we give to him. Evil exists. It cannot have power in this world unless it finds a consenting person to do his bidding. Our children do not need to fear Satan. They need to understand he will do everything he can to disable them and keep them out of the front lines in the body of Christ. They need help seeing how Satan is devouring the other children of their generation. They need to know that God intends to use them in their world with all the sin and temptations. They need to know that Jesus Christ will be at their side every single solitary moment of the battle if he is invited.

Brent Curtis writes, “Indeed, one of Satan’s most powerful whisperings to us is that we are expendable. He may admit we are part of God’s plan for his own glory but only in the same way Napoleon used his soldiers to establish his empire.” [4] One of the areas I am continually alarmed about is the way that different forms of media teach our children values. TV teaches our children that they are not all right just as they are created. There is a whole list of advertised products to make them more desirable as people. Sensuality in advertising is commonplace. Ron Hutchcraft asserts that, “No generation has ever grown up amid the sex-saturated bombardment these children have faced from early ages. It seems almost impossible for many of them to go even a few minutes without sexual thoughts.” [5]

Internet pornography entices and addicts more of our children every day. All of the screens our children have access to watch via TV, Computer, Internet, and Video games have a tremendous potential to teach. And they are designed to grab the attention of the emotional brain that operates below the critical thinking. Continued stimulation to the attention center raises the flight or fight hormones which has a deleterious impact on the child. The myriads of screens in the world are tremendously powerful in their ability to entice our children and build strongholds. When I think of the power of the illuminated screen it gives a new context of meaning to 2 Corinthians 11:14 when it says, “And no wonder, for Satan himself masquerades as an angel of light.”

CONSEQUENCES OF SIN

The underlying premise to teach your children about all of sin is that sin has consequences. God makes the rules. He is a loving God. He is an incredibly merciful God. But, God makes the rules.

There are a few truths that simply do not change. The

first is that there is a God and Creator. The second is that God has designed His laws into His creation. Interestingly, we seem to forget this. We fail to train our children that there are defined laws and that violation of those laws will have consequences. We have a God that will not be mocked.

We can sit on the fence, but guess what? God and His laws are the same whether we believe He is there or not. If I am pondering whether a mass in a young man's neck is cancer, the reality of what it is does not change based on what I decide. If it is cancer it will continue to grow despite my reassurance.

Sometimes I use the metaphor that God's Truth is a lot like a bucket of water. It is simple. It is straightforward. It is real and tangible. We can splash around in that bucket and try to make it look different. We can stir it and add frills. But it remains a bucket of water in its simplicity. The poem "The Indispensable Man" describes the bucket this way,

> "You may splash all you want when you enter;
> You may stir up water galore.
> But stop, and you'll find that in no time,
> It looks quite the same as before."[6]

God is an unchanging ever-present God. Who He is does not change because we discuss and dispute His presence. The laws that He has designed into creation are there whether we propose evolution as the basis of all life or stand in awe of our Creator. The laws are the same regardless of our debates. They are unchanging. They are not evolving. They are they same today as they were on the day of creation.

Somewhere, in each of our homes we should hang Galatians 6:7-8 that says, "Do not be deceived: God cannot be mocked. A man reaps what he sows. The one who sows to please the sinful nature, from the nature will reap destruction; the one who sows to please the Spirit, from the Spirit will reap eternal life."

Earnie Larsen, a popular speaker here in the Twin City area, has been trying to communicate this message for years. In the last twenty years, I have directed many patients toward his books, audiotapes and conferences. He explains:

> "What you live with; you learn.
> What you learn; you practice.
> What you practice; you become.
> And what you become has consequences." [7]

We have learned from the brain development information that the brain learns to imitate and internalize what it sees, hears and experiences. It lays down neural networks based on its experiences. What you have learned, you then become. It is from what you place on the throne of your heart that your motivations for all of life will emerge. Finally, our children have to understand that what they choose to become will have consequences.

There is a consequence to all of sin. When we put man on the throne we are forever seeking approval and needing to do a better dance. We never feel loved. When the self is on the throne we become addicted to our indulgences and the addictions begin to feel like slavery and shackles. Don't let your children be lulled into the thinking of the world. Sin has definite painful consequences.

The biggest consequence of sin is that it breaks our relationship with God. The next consequence is that it also strains and breaks our other relationships. The breakdown of our important relationships drives us into incredible loneliness and we keep trying to fill the void with more of the poisons from the world.

The other teachable truth about consequences is that sometimes our children will not see or feel them immediately. But, they are real and they are there. Josh

McDowell states, "The evidence of Truth does not pretend that morality is always rewarded and immorality is always punished. It simply views God's moral imperatives as furnishing an umbrella of protection and provision under which the wise will seek shelter. As we have said earlier, sin promotes immediate satisfaction and does often deliver pleasure for a season. Some of the consequences of sin or rewards for righteousness may not be measured out until after this life." [8]

CHAPTER 10

BREAKING STRONGHOLDS

This area is the most intriguing for me to write. I have witnessed in my twenty years of medical practice many success stories. I have seen incredible brokenness in people transform into strength. Over and over I have seen the power of God's Word in breaking strongholds. The basic premise for breaking any stronghold is to place God's TRUTH in the place of the lies in our neural networks.

If we look closely at the way that Jesus dispelled Satan we will see that He accomplished this with the Word of God. Matthew 4: 4 "Jesus answered, 'It is written: 'Man does not live on bread alone but on every word that comes from the mouth of God.'"

Matthew 4:9-10 " 'All this I will give you,' he said, 'if you will bow down and worship me.' Jesus said to him, 'Away from me, Satan! For it is written: 'Worship the Lord your God, and serve him only.' "

All of us will be tempted. All of us will falter and fail. But, there is a way beyond the patterns. There is victory over the addiction pathways that establish in the brain. 1 Peter 5:10 "And the God of all grace, who called you to his eternal glory in Christ, after you have suffered a little while, **will himself restore you** and make you strong, firm and steadfast." (My emphasis added.)

In Matthew 5:44 Jesus encourages us to not allow strongholds develop in the first place! He says, "Love your enemies and pray for those who persecute you." Remember the chapter on wounds? If we allow the arrows that are aimed at us to find a deep spot in the brain it will continue to grow and fester. If we understand the effects of the arrows in our neural networks we will see more easily that Satan is the keeper of the arrows. When we see the big picture it becomes surprisingly easy to pray for the individual Satan chooses as his archer. Remember, once we recognize the lies of Satan and bring them into the light of God's truth, the arrows have no power in our neural networks. They are kept in a proper perspective and the truth is maintained! Pray for those who persecute you. They are under the control of the Keeper of the Arrows. They are in desperate need of prayer right now!

Finally, in our talk about breaking strongholds, I want you to think outside the box with me for a moment. Does it ever amaze you that words on a page, God's Words, have so much power? Why don't the words on the pages of a self-help book have the same incredible transforming results? As I have studied the body and the brain I have come to stand in awe of its creator. I stand even more in awe that our creator chooses to have a very intimate personal relationship with us.

Let's trace back. We saw how perfectly God has programmed the body to fit the precepts of the soul. The behavior and thoughts that are the results of our sin cause increasing stress levels in the brain and body. These lower the immune system and lead to cell death and the ultimate death of the body. The price we pay for sin is death. It's programmed into us. Beautiful things are also programmed into the human person. Brain cells for empathy are there at birth. We have an experience of joy when we see beauty. In this way, we are programmed to see and recognize God in the form of beauty.

All through the body God has shown us that His design contains keys and locks. Everything in the body works through receptors and the perfectly matched molecule that will bring it to life. I became even more intrigued by the power of the Word of God when the research about music showed that we actually are born with the ability to recognize shapes or contours of music, not just notes or vibrations. The brain is designed to recognize a 'contour' to music. This is similar to the lock and key pattern in the cells but on a much grander scale. We are actually designed to recognize bigger shapes of things.

Could it be that our brains our designed in a way that the Word of God has a perfect fit in the 'lock'? Could it be that the reason the Word is grace is because once the Word of God is given its proper place in our neural networks that it releases our brain from the control of those addictive neural networks? Could it be that "the law" that Jesus talks about that He has power over is partly this law that exists in our human cells?

In the *New Living Translation* Matthew 11:28-30 says, "Come to me, all of you who are weary and carry heavy burdens, and I will give you rest. Take my yoke upon you. Let me teach you, because I am humble and gentle, and you will find rest for your souls. **For my yoke fits perfectly,** and the burden I give you is light." (My emphasis)

Why is God so careful to tell us that Jesus is "The Word"? John 1:14 "The Word became flesh and made His dwelling among us." John 1:17, "For the law was given through Moses; grace and truth came through Jesus Christ."

Could there be even a bigger picture here in God's

design? Are we designed for the Word of God to fit perfectly in our minds? Could this be part of the design of Christ's incredible healing power? John 3:36 "Whoever believes in the Son has eternal life, but whoever rejects the Son will not see life, for God's wrath remains on him."

John 6:63 "The Spirit gives life; the flesh counts for nothing. The words I have spoken to you are spirit and they are life."

John 8:24 "I told you that you would die in your sins; if you do not believe that I am the one I claim to be, you will indeed die in your sins."

John 8: 34 "Jesus replied, 'I tell you the truth, everyone who sins is a slave to sin.' "

John 10:4 "When he has brought out all his own, he goes on ahead of them, and his sheep follow him because they know his voice." Has God designed the human person to recognize the shape of His Word the same way we are designed to recognize the shape of music?

John 12:49-50 "For I did not speak of my own accord, but the Father who sent me commanded me what to say and how to say it. I know that his command leads to eternal life. So, whatever I say is just what the Father has told me to say."

John 15:7 " If you remain in me and my words remain in you, ask whatever you wish and it will be given to you." What is this amazing power of the Word of God within the human person?

John 16:35 "I have told you these things, so that in me you may have peace. In this world you will have trouble. But, take heart! I have overcome the world."

John 17:25-26 "Righteous Father, though the world does not know you, I know you, and they know that you have sent me. I have made you known to them, and will continue to make you known in order that the love you have for me may be in them and **that I myself may be in them."** (My emphasis)

John 14:16-17 "And I will ask the Father, and he will give you another Counselor to be with you forever-the Spirit of truth. The world cannot accept him, because it neither sees him nor knows him. But you know him, **for he lives with you and will be in you.**" (My emphasis.)

Acts 20:32 "Now I commit you to God and to the word of his grace, which can build you up and give you an inheritance among all those who are sanctified." How does His Word become grace among all the foolishness of our decisions? How does His Word provide grace for the healing of addictions? It is real. Anyone struggling with addictions can attest to the incredible power of God's Word in healing those pathways.

Romans 6:14 "For sin shall not be your master, because you are not under law, but under grace."

Colossians 2:2-3 "My purpose is that they may be encouraged in heart and united in love, so that they may have the full riches of complete understanding, in order that they may know the mystery of God, namely Christ, in whom are hidden all the treasures of wisdom and knowledge."

Many verses tell us that God's Word is flawless. See 2 Sam 22:31, Proverbs 30:5, Psalm 12:6, and Psalm 119:160. Jesus stated several times that His Words were not His, they came from God the Father. Proverbs warns us in Proverbs 30:6 not to change God's Word. "Do not add to his words, or he will rebuke you and prove you a liar."

His Word, in exactly the shape and form He wants it given to us, is meant to live in us. His word is grace. It is truth. It is spirit. It is eternal.

We are again warned in the last chapter of Revelation that God's Word cannot have its form changed!

Revelation 22:19 says, "And if anyone takes words away from this book of prophecy, God will take away from him his share in the tree of life and in the holy city, which are described in this book."

Hebrews 4:12 "For the Word of God is living and active. Sharper than any double-edged sword, it penetrates even to dividing soul and spirit, joints and marrow, it judges the thoughts and attitudes of the heart."

This concept gives us much to ponder in our hearts. For me, it offers a great deal of comfort in knowing God may have designed a key place for Himself inside this human body. It also gives me a bigger framework to place the incredible significance of God's Word and the almost incomprehensible meaning to what Jesus Christ accomplished for us through His death. It also creates in me a fresh importance to bringing God's Word into the hearts of those who are wounded. It gives renewed importance to bringing God's Word into the developing mind of our children.

CHAPTER 11

PRAYER

The last chapter on breaking strongholds brings us naturally into a discussion of prayer. Prayer is an incredible privilege. Surprisingly, many of us understand the power of prayer; yet, we spend very little time praying. Is it because we don't really feel we can 'hear' God's voice when He is trying to teach us? Perhaps we have never witnessed the aliveness of prayer or recognized the answers when they arrive.

Most of us could give many examples to demonstrate answered prayer. Two stand out in my mind because they demonstrate very different components of prayer. I have often prayed that God will reveal Himself to my children, so they will know He is real and not struggle for many years of their lives trying to 'get it'. The first example demonstrates prayer when we are desperate but it astounded my children with God's realness.

I was driving across Northern Wisconsin in a blinding blizzard. I was alone with my boys then five and seven years old. About an hour into the white-knuckle drive my 'stress hormones' stimulated my heart and I developed a very irregular heartbeat. As I started to feel more light-headed, I realized there was nowhere to pull over. And as I rolled down the window for cold air, I also realized that any stopping on the highway would make us a target for any approaching, also 'blinded,' drivers. I told the kids we had to pray. Now, God may have answered that prayer in many ways such as ending my arrhythmia. But, He chose, within seconds, to stop the snow completely from the moment we uttered that desperate prayer. We were all speechless. Why did I wait until I was desperate?

Well, three years passed. Again I was in the car alone with my boys now eight and ten. We had been traveling for a little over 12 hours in driving rain. The road spray alone made the drive exhausting to try to see the highways. We were trying to get to a destination another five hours away. My boys were very excited and set on arriving that day so they could see my sister before she had to leave the next morning. I decided to start preparing them that once darkness fell, I probably wouldn't be able to see to keep driving. A cry of disappointment gushed from both boys. My youngest, in his innocence, said, "Mom we didn't even pray about it." As I looked in front of me at the hundreds of miles of black storm clouds hovering over the Great Lakes I knew prayer would be hopeless. How could I use this as a 'teachable moment'? Maybe, I could teach them about how sometimes God says no, yes or wait.

Before I could respond, Matthew said with dismay; "Well if you won't pray, I will." Both boys started praying. I felt like I had let them down as a mother. Within about 5 miles the skies cleared and we did not have another drop of rain during the trip. And as I continued to drive God very quietly whispered into my heart, "You wouldn't even ask." We set limits on God!

How much of your prayer life is spent in desperate times? How many of the burdens and trials of life do you carry alone without prayer? How many times do we as parents place limits on God because we can't possibly see the way out? Why are you limiting God? Are you like me, afraid to be disappointed? Are you afraid His silence may only raise your doubts about His realness? Is there an area with one of your children in which you have given up hope? Jesus Christ is the master of Hope! Instead of despair, why not get many people praying for the struggles your child is having? God loves our children even more than we do. We have to ask!

Powerful strongholds have been brought down by prayer, especially by praying God's Word in prayer. Ron Hutchcraft wrote, "Through prayer, we access God's power to open hearts that would otherwise be closed…to open doors that otherwise would never open…to change hearts that have resisted every other force…to experience God's wisdom in making decisions that affect our lives and others." [1]

Remember 2 Chronicles 16:9 "For the eyes of the LORD range throughout the earth to strengthen those whose hearts are fully committed to him." At some point we have to get off the fence and make the conscious commitment to God. We need to recognize the end of our strength and come back to Him. Our time in the lives of our children is really very short. And the opportunities for building and developing the spiritual pathways are also limited. The battle is too intense to try to parent without the power of prayer. It is time. Start building a powerful prayer campaign for the teaching, the provision, and the protection of your children.

There have been volumes written on prayer. I won't attempt what they have already accomplished. I will simply bring three areas into focus. First, what the Bible teaches us about prayer; secondly, some approaches to praying for our children; and finally, what some famous people have said about prayer over the ages.

Other than the Lord's Prayer, I think Matthew 7:7-8 describes prayer the most completely. In that verse Jesus himself tells us, "Ask and it will be given to you;

seek and you will find; knock and the door will be opened to you. For everyone who asks, receives; he who seeks finds; and to him who knocks, the door will be opened."

Luke 1:37 says, "For nothing is impossible with God."

Matthew 6:7-8 "And when you pray, do not keep on babbling like pagans, for they think they will be heard because of their many words. Do not be like them, for your Father knows what you need before you ask Him."

James 1: 5-6 "If any of you lacks wisdom, he should ask God, who gives generously to all without finding fault, and it will be given to him. But, when he asks, he must believe and not doubt, because he who doubts is like a wave of the sea, blown and tossed by the wind."

James 4:3 "When you ask, you do not receive, because you ask with the wrong motives, that you may spend what you get on your pleasures."

One way to have an active prayer life is to make time for God every single day. Remember how we need to constantly renew our minds so we can tell those neural networks what is important? Read God's Word. There is immeasurable wisdom and power there. Don't just hear the word; obey it. In other words pray for the grace to be able to walk your talk. Our children are watching us live. It is only through grace and prayer that we can become a role model of integrity. It is only through the constant indwelling Holy Spirit that we can own on the inside what we model on the outside.

Jesus Christ desires to walk with us. He asks us to take up His yoke so that He can share the burden. Matthew 11:28-30 says "Come to me, all you who are weary and burdened, and I will give you rest. Take my yoke upon you and learn from me, for I am gentle and humble in heart and you will find rest for your souls. For my yoke is easy and my burden is light."

Psalm 34: 18-19 "The Lord is close to the broken-hearted and saves those who are crushed in spirit. A righteous man may have many troubles, but the Lord delivers him from them all."

Pray for the character development of your children. For example, if your child is struggling with unkindness pray this verse for them. I Thessalonians 5:15 “Make sure that nobody pays back wrong for wrong, but always try to be kind to each other and to everyone else.” Pray that the character traits that God desires in our children will be those with the strongest neural networks. Find the verses that support those character traits. Give them lots of opportunities to demonstrate Godly traits and reinforce them when you see them in your child's behavior. The pathways in the brain that are used most often will be the strongest.

Finally, we need to teach them to pray. Pray together every day. Pay attention to their heart as they learn to pray. Encourage a thankful heart so that they can always approach God with the full understanding of how much they have been given! Encourage them to pray for others and to recognize the hurting hearts around them. Help them see God in their world. Pray for missionaries and share their stories with thanksgiving for the hand of God alive and active in their lives.

Help them pray with real meaning for what their needs and fears are. Praise God when we receive answers to prayer so they might see Him work. Remember, Satan will work overtime to distract them and fill them with doubts about the realness of prayer and God. We need to be a strong buffer to our children and stand firm. Seek out a prayer partner who will pray with you for your child. We need to seek out other Godly adult role models in the lives of our children.

Why pray? David Butts at the Kansas Christian Church wrote, “But people don't pray because they believe in prayer. They pray because they believe in God. If people do believe that He is the all-powerful God of the Bible, who has not put His power on hold – then they will pray.” [2] He also explains that, “Our trust in the power of God continues not because we always get our way, but because we believe in the way of God.” [3]

E. LeRoy Lawson, President of Pacific Christian College wrote, "Our prayer, then, is to make ourselves instruments of his benevolent desires on earth, to team up with him against the countervailing forces of evil." [4] Remember, our relationship with God is much like our relationships with our children. When those relationships are wounded we need to come back to them and ask forgiveness. Nothing is more important than those relationships. Cherish the one you have with our Lord Jesus. And, protect at all costs those you are developing with your children.

One final idea from David Eubanks, President of Johnson Bible College: "One can study the Bible without praying, but no one can be successful in prayer without the Word, which is the foundation of all prayer." [5]

Let's conclude the section on prayer with a few of the quotes from famous people about prayer. General Robert E. Lee wrote " Knowing that intercessory prayer is our mightiest weapon and the supreme call for all Christians today, I pleadingly urge our people everywhere to pray. Believing that prayer is the greatest contribution that our people can make in this critical hour, I humbly urge that we take time to pray – to really pray." [6]

In 1980 Ronald Reagan stated, "The time has come to turn to God and reassert our trust in Him for the healing of America...our country is in need of and ready for a spiritual renewal." [7] In 1984 Mr. Reagan wisely commented, "America was founded by people who believed that God was their rock of safety. I recognize we must be cautious in claiming that God is on our side, but I think it's all right to keep asking if we're on His side." [8]

Finally, Alexander Solzhenitsyn, a famous Russian author, stated in 1983, "Instead of the ill-advised hopes of the last two centuries, which have reduced us to insignificance and brought us to the brink of nuclear and non-nuclear death, we can only reach with determination for the warm hand of God, which we have so rashly and self-confidently pushed away." [9]

CHAPTER 12

The SPIRITUAL ARMOR

What is the Christian armor all about anyway? Is it possible to truly teach a child to understand it? Do you believe there is a spiritual battle? We'll approach this concept of a spiritual battle first and then we will discuss the armor.

One of the first steps in the spiritual battle is to decide whom you will serve. Matthew 6:26 explains that, "No one can serve two masters." Joshua was also very clear about this. "Choose for yourself this day whom you will serve. As for me and my house, we will serve the Lord." Read the full passage closely. Joshua 24:15: "But if serving the Lord seems undesirable to you, then choose for yourself this day whom you will serve, whether the gods your forefathers served beyond the River, or the gods of the Amorites, in whose land you are living. But as for me and my household, we will serve the Lord." The point is that staying on the fence is a conscious choice not to serve our Lord! The throne of our heart is never empty. If Christ is not there, either the esteem of man or the satisfaction of the flesh will be.

The second step is to understand what you will use for armor. The world offers us many alternatives to spiritual armor, such as was offered to David by King Saul. Before he went into battle against Goliath, Saul offered David the royal armor. Remember this story from 1 Samuel 17: 38-39? "Then Saul dressed David in his own tunic. He put a coat of armor on him and a bronze helmet on his head. David fastened on his sword over the tunic and tried walking around, because he was not used to them. 'I cannot go in these,' he said to Saul, 'because I am not used to them,' so he took them off." David chose to enter battle with his spiritual armor.

The third step is to make a commitment. In each child's life, there needs to be a time of conscious commitment to Jesus Christ. This is what we talked about at the beginning as the 'sealing the soda can.' At that moment, they give total control of their life to Jesus through the person of His Holy Spirit. They make a conscious choice to wear the armor. As parents, we do the training. We present them with the Word of God in a way they can understand. We live in a way that the power of the Holy Spirit is visible in us, so they can learn who He is. Ultimately our children have to choose to wear the armor.

The fourth step is to survey the battlefield. Somehow the world has filled the minds of our children with the notion that life should be easy. They are led to believe that when life gets tough, they are probably in the wrong place. This lie is preached whether it is their marriage, schoolwork, their job or an important relationship. As your child learns to survey the battlefield, use that pep talk again about the NBA game. There is nowhere in God's Word that promises them that this will be easy. There are many places that tell us it will be hard.

Beth Moore wisely reminds us that, "Difficulty does not necessarily mean disaster. Heavy winds and raging seas don't always mean you're on the wrong course." [1] Matthew 7:13-14 tells us to "Enter through the narrow gate. For wide is the gate and broad is the road that leads to destruction, and many enter through it. But small is the gate and narrow the road that leads to life, and only a few find it." Remember the word picture Jesus painted in Matthew 10:16? "I am sending you out like sheep among wolves."

What God does promise us is that He will equip us completely.

1 Corinthian 10:13 promises "No temptation has seized you except that what is common to man. And God is faithful; he will not let you be tempted beyond what you can bear. But when you are tempted, he will also provide a way out so that you can stand up under it." 2 Timothy 1:7 "But God did not give us a spirit of timidity, but a spirit of power, of love and of self-discipline."

The final step is to be very clear why we are in the battle. Finally, our children have to have a very clear idea of why they are in the battle. What are they defending? 2 Timothy 1:14 says to "Guard the good deposit that was entrusted to you – guard it with the help of the Holy Spirit who lives in us." Proverbs 4:23 says, "Above all else, guard your heart, for it is the well-spring of life." There are very precious spritual truths that we need to train our children to guard. However, our children also have the choice to decide if they will enter the battle from the offense or the defense.

You see, we train our children to recognize the traps of the world, and they learn to focus on Satan. Even from the brain development perspective, it is more effective to teach a child what they should do rather than what they shouldn't. The battle is not about Satan. The battle is about choosing Christ. The authors of *The Sacred Romance* offer us rich insight:

> God's intention, on the other hand, is to use spiritual warfare to draw us into deeper communion with Himself. Satan's device is to isolate us and wear us out obsessing about what he has done and what he will do next. And, he is very effective in using our particular Message of the Arrows to do it. God desires to use the enemy's attacks to remove the obstacles between ourselves and him; to reestablish our dependency on him as his sons and daughters in a much deeper way. Once we understand that, the warfare we are in begins to feel totally different. It is not really even about Satan anymore, but about communion with God and abiding in Jesus as the source of life. [2]

If the reason for battle was merely to survive, we could keep them in their bubble wrap; but the person of Jesus Christ is so much bigger! There is a world of hurting people out there. They need what our children have. Ron Hutchcraft summarizes it this way:

> If the goal for our Christian young people is merely to survive, they probably won't. Survival is an unworthy goal for a person in whom there lives Resurrection Power! No, they don't need a survival kit. They need a mission. [3]

But God did not give us a spirit of timidity, but a spirit of power, of love and of self-discipline. 2 Timothy 1:7

THE CHRISTIAN ARMOR IS DESCRIBED IN EPHESIANS 6: 10-20. It is worth rereading it in context before going into the separate parts.

The Spiritual Armor

Stand firm then, with the belt of truth buckled around your waist, with the breastplate of righteousness in place, and with your feet fitted with the readiness that comes from the gospel of peace. In addition to all this, take up the shield of faith, with which you can extinguish all the flaming arrows of the evil one. Take the helmet of salvation and the sword of the spirit, which is the word of God.

Ephesians 6:14-17

Verse 6:14 - **"the belt of truth wrapped around your waist."** This ties the armor all together. Remember our premise that anything that is not God's truth Satan will use? Only God's Truth has the real power in this battle. It is the basis for everything. Every stronghold gets built on the basis of lies. Teach your children to cling to the Truth. It is a lifeline.

Verse 6:14: **"with the breastplate of righteousness in place."** This breastplate is meant to protect the heart, the center of emotions and the wellspring of life. The emotional center of the body gives all meaning and passion to life. The emotional center of the body is our motivation for all of our actions. Matthew 6:21 says, "For where your treasure is, there your heart will be also." If a love for Jesus Christ lies at the center of our emotions, He is our treasure.

For our children, explaining the protection of the breastplate also means explaining God's precepts for right and wrong. He has set his standards in place to protect their hearts. His laws are the real breastplate. Wearing the breastplate means they have made a decision to remain within the boundaries God set up! James 1:22 says, "Do not merely listen to the word, and so deceive yourselves. Do what it says." If there is no fear of the Lord in the hearts of our children, there will be no self-control. We can easily discern who occupies the throne of our child's heart by the way they live, treat people, and what they let into their brains through media.

Above all else, guard your heart, for it is the well-spring of life. Proverbs 4:23

Guide your children through this area. It is a minefield! Help them spot the counterfeits. Teach them discernment. It will be an active process at every phase of their brain development. Find ways to reinforce to them that God is real. We don't make Him up. His laws, as we have learned through sin's effects on the body, are real as well.

> When they reject truth as an objective standard, their view of life becomes distorted. When their view becomes distorted they easily accept counterfeits. When they accept counterfeits, they begin to make wrong choices. When then they make wrong choices they suffer the consequences. The choice is, quite literally, truth or consequences. [4]

Verse 6:15 - **"and with your feet fitted with the readiness that comes from the gospel of peace."** This part of the armor gives them their mission. They need to prepare their minds and feet for action. Their hearts can be completely overflowing with love for Jesus Christ; but they also have to give control of their feet to Jesus as well. Teach them to recognize his voice. Teach them to trust God. If He opens a door, He wants them there. 1 Peter 1:13 "Therefore, prepare your minds for action; be self-controlled; set your hope fully on the grace to be given you when Jesus is revealed."

Verse 6:16 - **"In addition to all this, take up the shield of faith, with which you can extinguish all the flaming arrows of the evil one."** This part is huge! The shield of faith actually exists in their minds, where they have come to learn and trust that God is real and will keep His promises. If the breastplate is God's precepts, the shield is God's promises.

When I first attempted to write this manuscript, I was astounded at the level of spiritual warfare I experienced. I was also amazed at how many arrows were able to penetrate my shield of faith. I realized that whenever God pushes us out of our comfort zone, there are always the doubts about whether we really heard God's voice correctly. We host the familiar debate about how much of this is really from God. Is part of this just from me? One morning God directed me to read and claim His Words in Revelation 3:7-8. It said, "These are the words of him who is holy and true, who holds the key of David. What he opens no one can shut, and what he shuts no one can open. I know your deeds. See, I have placed before you an open door that no one can shut. I know that you have little strength, yet you have kept my word and have not denied my name." Once I understood that verse, I started to recognize the arrows, and I used that verse to tighten my hold on the shield.

Beth Moore reinforces this well:

> Satan will stop at nothing to get us to lower our shield of faith so he can wound and burn us. He stacks up tangible evidence in opposition to God's assurances. He delights in doubts and lies. He studies our weaknesses and then aims where we are vulnerable. His priority job description is to keep us from believing God....first, for salvation, and then for completion." [5]

1 Peter 1:5: "Who through faith are shielded by God's power until the coming of the salvation that is ready to be revealed in the last time."

Philippians 1:6: "being confident of this, that he who began a good work in you will carry it on to completion until the day of Christ Jesus."

1 Thessalonians 5:24: "The one who calls you is faithful and he will do it."

Verse 6: 17 - **"take the helmet of salvation."** Our salvation through Christ Jesus allowed for Satan to be defeated. The ultimate power of the helmet of salvation is that we now have the power to break strongholds that develop in our thought processes. We now have the power through the power of Jesus Christ to forgive the deep inner emotional wounds.

Take captive every thought to make it obedient to Christ.

2 Corinthians 10:5

The nature of that forgiveness is divine and transcendent, as anyone who has faced that journey can testify. 2 Corinthians 2:11 talks about forgiveness "in order that Satan might not outwit us. For we are not unaware of his schemes."

Having the helmet of salvation is such an unbelievably powerful gift! Because Jesus died, salvation also comes in the form of what His Living Word can now do in our minds. The Bible describes the Word of God as a double-edged sword. It provides an offense, as we will explore next in the sword of the Spirit; but it also provides a defense. It does this through its ability to protect our neural networks and bring down strongholds. We would not have access to any of this had not Christ died. He is God's Word. 1 John 1:17 says, "For the law was given through Moses; grace and truth came through Jesus Christ." The helmet of salvation is our grace. It is also Truth.

2 Corinthians 10:5 reminds us to "Take captive every thought to make it obedient to Christ." Let His spirit control our thoughts as we wear His helmet of salvation. Remember, the quote from Earnie Larsen? "What you live with, you learn; what you learn, you practice; what you practice, you become and what you become, has consequences."[6] If we live with Jesus Christ as the core of our thoughts; we learn His ways. Once we learn His ways; we practice them. Once we practice them; we become like Him. And once we become like Him; we are transformed! And, that has consequences!

When we wear the helmet of salvation we become transformed by the inner dwelling of Christ in our neural networks. 2 Corinthians 3:17-18 "Now the LORD is the Spirit, and where the Spirit of the LORD is, there is freedom. And we, who with unveiled faces all reflect the LORD's glory, are being transformed into his likeness with ever increasing glory, which comes from the LORD, who is the Spirit."

Once we recognize the incredible gift of salvation, the helmet also reminds us to keep a focus on what's important and what's eternal. We need to keep the minds of our children uncluttered from life's nonessentials. This is a trap for our children through the glut of media options that vie for their minds.

Remember that spiritual truths are revealed. Jesus Christ chooses to reveal them. Matthew 11:27 "no one really knows the Father except the Son and those to whom the Son chooses to reveal him."

Wearing the helmet of salvation will also give us the mind of Christ as we approach our world and listen to where he wants us. It gives us the mind of Christ to be discerning about subtle strongholds in our thought lives.

Take the time to continually renew the mind and remind yourself how essential that helmet of salvation is for us as Christians and for our children.

One way you might approach the helmet of salvation with a younger child is to continually strengthen the neural networks that understand creation. Help them know that God loves them. Demonstrate this through the unconditional love you shower them with at home. Let them know their salvation was bought at a price. There is great worth to their soul. Let them know that salvation is a gift. They cannot earn it, but, they must choose to accept it by wearing the helmet. Remind them that they are here, right now, for a purpose; God's purpose. Above all, partner with the Holy Spirit to use that helmet to protect their minds.

"Not by might nor by power, but by my Spirit," says the LORD Almighty.

Zechariah 4:6

The mind is the inroad Satan will use to steal and destroy what has already been bought. It should come as no surprise that every TV producer, product advertiser, video-game maker, and cigarette manufacturer wants a piece of your child's mind as well.

Verse 6:17 - **"and the sword of the Spirit, which is the word of God."** When we teach our children about the sword of the Spirit, we can present the offensive part of the double-edged sword. Where the helmet protected, the sword will provide. Zechariah 4:6 " 'Not by might nor by power, but by my Spirit,' says the LORD Almighty." God has a plan. We can trust Him to direct our ways. Ephesians 1:22-23 explains that plan. "And God placed all things under his feet and appointed him to be head over everything for the church, which is his body, the fullness of him who fills everything in every way." Trust Him to guide you in every way. Psalm 119:105 "Your word is a lamp to my feet and a light for my path." The guidance of the Holy Spirit through the Word of God is the best offense.

Finally, cover your child in prayer continually. Remember, the armor is only complete when it is surrounded and protected by prayer.

CHAPTER 13

INTERNET PORNOGRAPHY

For parents at the start of the 21st century, the availability of Internet pornography has loomed into a tremendous beast. In my 20 years of medical practice, I have never seen the times change so radically as they have since the Internet became widely available.

My own personal journey with the beast began about two years ago when I reported two cases of child sexual abuse in the same week. This incidence alone was unusual. What really sparked my attention, however, was that the abuse occurred in two separate cities by 14-year-old boys addicted to Internet pornography. Their victims were younger children. My first patient was a 5-year-old girl. The second child was an 8-year-old boy. When I called to report the second case I asked the police officer what was happening here. He assured me I had only seen the tip of the iceberg!

This explosion of pornography has taken most of us parents off guard. Many of us had not yet completed the teaching about healthy sexuality with our children before we had to equip our children to understand the trap of pornography. The problem only became more complicated as we realized that many public libraries do not filter pornography from the computers accessed by our children.

This sudden appearance of the beast is particularly alarming because the adolescent brain is unusually susceptible to addiction. A deep heaviness filled my heart to realize the magnitude of the numbers of children who could become shackled by an addiction to pornography. Addictions become deeply rooted when they establish themselves in the brain when the child is developing. This is when they need to be forming their neural networks for a 'healthy' sexual response. Stephen Arterburn writes:

> In nearly every case we've dealt with, the use of pornography began when the people were adolescents. If children make it out of adolescence without being heavily exposed to pornography, they most likely won't develop a problem with it later on. [1]

My purpose in covering Internet pornography is to offer you resources as parents. We will discuss how addictions form in the developing minds of our children. Then we'll try to create a bigger perspective on the problem to help us find ways to keep the beast out. One of the most frustrating parts of the problem for parents is that pornographic images stay very deeply etched in the minds of children because they deliver such a strong emotional jolt as the child views it. The more strongly that a child responds emotionally to an event; the deeper the event will leave a neural imprint! We talked about this with the amygdala when we discussed emotional wounds as well as the effects of TV.

Do you not know that your bodies are members of Christ himself?
1 Corinthians 6:15

Let's back up and get a perspective. We started off this journey by examining the timeline from the Fall of the Roman Empire. Let's take a quick look at why it fell. Francis Schaeffer states:

> Edward Gibbon (1737-1794) in his "Decline and Fall of the Roman Empire" (1776-1788) said the following five attributes marked Rome at its end: First, a mounting love of show and luxury (that is, affluence); second, a widespread gap between the very rich and the very poor....third, an obsession with sex; fourth, freakishness in the arts, masquerading as originality, and enthusiasm pretending to be creativity; fifth, an increased desire to live off the state. [2]

It is very interesting that the Fall of the Roman Empire was marked, at least in part, by an obsession with sex. **Have you ever wondered what is so incredibly special and unique about God's design for human sexuality that Satan would battle for it so ferociously?** Why can Satan's control of sexuality lead to the fall of a powerful Empire? What was happening inside that culture? Is it happening within ours?

One of the key things we need to understand to keep sexuality in perspective is that God considers our body to be His temple. He has perfectly designed it for His Spirit to reside here. While He was alive Jesus referred to His own body as a temple in John 2:19: "Jesus answered them, 'Destroy this temple, and I will raise it again in three days.'"

"The point to decide is this – "Do I agree with my Lord and Master that my body shall be His temple?" If so, then for me the whole of the law for the body is summed up in this revelation, that my body is the temple of the Holy Ghost" [3]

Other verses also emphasize that this concept of a temple is for real and to be taken very seriously. 1Corinthians provides specific instruction.

- 1 Corinthians 3: 16: "Don't you know that you yourselves are God's temple and that God's Spirit lives in you? If anyone destroys God's temple, God will destroy him; for God's temple is sacred, and you are that temple."

- 1 Corinthians 6:13: "The body is not meant for sexual immorality, but for the Lord, and the Lord for the body."

- 1 Corinthians 6:15: "Do you not know that your bodies are members of Christ himself?"

- 1 Corinthians 6:18-20: "Flee from sexual immorality. All other sins a man commits are outside his body, but he who sins sexually sins against his own body. Do you not know that your body is a temple of the Holy Spirit, who is in you, whom you have received from God? You are not your own; you were bought at a price. Therefore, honor God with your body."

- 1 Corinthians 6:16: "Do you not know that he who unites himself with a prostitute is one with her in body? For it is said, 'The two will become one flesh.' But he who unites himself with the Lord is one with him in spirit."

Sexual sin brings something detestable into God's temple. It can be no other way because sexual sin unites us with another person. What happens when we bring a detestable thing into our bodies? We will be set apart for destruction. Deuteronomy 7:26 tries to warn us about this process. It admonishes, "Do not bring a detestable thing into your house, or you, like it, will be set apart for destruction. Utterly abhor and detest it, for it is set apart for destruction."

Matthew records Jesus' teaching on this topic in 5:27-29 "You have heard that it was said, 'Do not commit adultery.' But I tell you that anyone who looks at a woman lustfully has already committed adultery with her in his heart. If your right eye causes you to sin, gouge it out and throw it away. It is better for you to lose one part of your body than for your whole body to be thrown into hell."

> Self-indulgence is absolutely insatiable. Lives given over to the passions of the flesh are never satisfied, and those who thirst for the perverse are never quenched. Self-indulgence is a never-ending cycle. [4]

Sexual sin is a really really big deal. It was part of the downfall of the powerful Roman Empire. It dramatically violates the temple of God's Spirit in us. And, it sets us on the conveyer belt set apart for destruction.

Proverbs 2:18-19 talks about being seduced by the wayward wife and says, "For her house leads down to death and her paths to the spirits of the dead. None who go to her return or attain the paths of life."

Proverbs 6 and Proverbs 7 are filled with warnings about sexual sin. Proverbs 6:26 describes that it "preys upon your very life."

Proverbs 7:23 describes the attractive lies on the road to sexual sin and the person, "Little knowing it will cost him his life."

The most chilling verses as we think of the sexual temptations available to our children today are Proverbs 7:24-27 "Now then, my sons, listen to me;

pay attention to what I say. Do not let your heart turn to her ways or stray into her paths. Many are the victims she has brought down; her slain are a mighty throng. Her house is a highway to the grave, leading down to the chambers of death."

GOD HAS A PLAN FOR SEXUALITY

God has a bigger plan for our sexuality. He is trustworthy!! Satan is well aware of God's plan. Satan is a robber. He comes to seduce us and our children. He intends to rob them of God's design for husband and wife sexual intimacy. Satan's battle is to take the transcendence out of our sexual intimacy.

God designed intimacy as a way for us to seek Him. When both sexual partners are alive in Christ, it is His spirit that flows and loves and exchanges during the sexual encounter. The authors of The Sacred Romance create a poignant picture of this process:

> The gospel says that we, who are God's beloved, created a cosmic crisis. It says we, too, were stolen from our True Love and that He launched the greatest campaign in the history of the world to get us back. God created us for intimacy with Him. [5]

"What He is after is us - our laughter, our tears, our dreams, our fears, our heart of hearts." [6]

We need to teach our children that God has designed the desire for intimacy as part of our sex drive Our desire for intimacy is really a desire for Him. Until they are able to understand this truth, all of their relationships will be fraught with frustration and failures. There is no partner on earth that could come close to meeting those emotional needs.

In nearly every case we've dealt with, the use of pornography began when the people were adolescents. If children make it out of adolescence without being heavily exposed to pornography, they most likely won't develop a problem with it later on. [8]

Contrary to our popular youth culture, the years of teen brain development need to be a time of emotional and spiritual maturation. If we neglect the spiritual, the emotional will never be balanced. As our teenagers learn to handle all the new emotions of adolescence, they also need to seek true intimacy with God. It's only when they recognize themselves as truly spiritual beings that the rest of the process follows without turmoil.

Sexual indulgence is a vile counterfeit. Look closely at how easily it carries Satan's counterfeit messages (lies) into the neural networks of our children. Look closely at how wounds happen and strongholds build in their hearts. Sexual indulgence fills us at the expense of taking from another. It is driven by our need to satisfy the flesh with instant gratification. It plants 'satisfaction of self' squarely on the throne of our life. It will tell any number of lies to obtain that satisfaction. We learn how to manipulate other people to meet our needs. Yet it leaves us barren, filled with shame, vulnerable to emotional wounding, and in need of more and more and more.

God's true desire for sexual intimacy is that it would be based on love and that He would be the originator of that creative energy. It draws from His Spirit. It brings truth into the neural networks instead of the lies. It allows us to love with the mind of Christ. We can focus on our beloved, instead of ourselves. We feel safe and satisfied. Frequently, we have weathered many storms together with Christ at the helm. Sexual intimacy flows from our daily trust and commitment. It is a gift. Love of this nature brings fruit into our lives rather than destruction. Love of this nature brings God's love into the world.

Our bodies were designed to experience sexual pleasure as a gift, not as bondage. Our body is designed for intimacy with one partner; the same way our spirit is designed for intimacy with one God.

Don't you know that you yourselves are God's temple and that God's Spirit lives in you? If anyone destroys God's temple, God will destroy him; for God's temple is sacred, and you are that temple.

1 Corinthians 3:16

IS THIS GENERATION LOST?

Certainly, a Christian parent can become easily discouraged by the elevated role that sex has in the media; but remember, sex is an "emotional jolt." The National Institute on Media and the Family reminds us that the motivation of the movie and TV industry is to sell the eyeballs of our children to advertisers. They need to keep the attention of our children.[9] To do this, they have created an industry that depicts sex as easy, fun, without consequences, enjoyable and filled with instant gratification. PBS produced a documentary titled *The Merchants of Cool*. In this video they reveal the calculated marketing utilized to keep children watching MTV. [10]

In 1998, Patricia Hersch wrote *A Tribe Apart*. Her chapter on teen sexuality was vividly accurate. She titled Chapter 10 "Sex: Let's get it out of the way, but don't look at me naked." [11] Satan comes to rob and steal. He is a thief.

When we teach our children about their sexuality remember what we have already covered about the emotional centers of the brain. Emotions are the greatest motivators of behavior. Many children are motivated by their loneliness to seek out sexual encounters where they are loved for the moment. We should be filling that loneliness factor in our homes with real relationships that they have with us and encourage their ongoing seeking of Jesus Christ. Many of our children view us as too busy. Especially at this critical age, parents need to be available and appear to have all the time in the world.

In my medical practice, the sexual dilemmas of children fill me with sadness. I'll almost always say something like, "Kim, we really need to talk to your mom about this." About 99% of the time the answer is always the same. "My mom is so busy, I don't want to add to her stress right now. She's working more at work because they just downsized."

"Kim I know your mom. She would quit her job if she knew you were struggling like this." Sometimes, "Kim" has a strong family that can pick up the pieces. Many times, she must deal with a family that has no reserves and the young woman's life quickly starts to unravel.

Do you not know that your body is a temple of the Holy Spirit, who is in you, whom you have received from God? You are not your own; you were bought at a price. Therefore, honor God with your body.

1 Corinthians 6:19-20

The only real motivation for abstinence will be your child's love for Jesus Christ. Their trust that He is real and keeps His promises will be the strongest emotional motivator in their life. Fear of disease or fear of pregnancy may motivate but not for long. It is their search for intimacy that will consume the teen years.

They will look for it in their peer group. They will look in sexual encounters. But God is not hiding! If they are encouraged to look for Him, they will find him.

Two years ago I had the privilege to attend one of Joshua Harris' "True Love" Seminars. For me, interacting with the youth at the conference was a life-changing experience. At his seminar held in Spooner, Wisconsin, I met a generation of teens on fire for Jesus Christ. I watched God raising up a generation willing to walk their talk. When I saw the aliveness of the Holy Spirit in their lives, I was flooded with an extra dose of hope. Jesus Christ is so real! We are selling our children short when we don't tell them the Truth about the power of the Holy Spirit!

As parents, we HAVE TO RECLAIM the power of the Holy Spirit for their lives and believe that He will do what He says he will do. We don't have to figure out the way to change their heart. HE DOES IT. We just have to walk with Christ and trust Him to transform our life into one that is worthy of being modeled. We have to show them that intimacy with God is real. It's not a 'metaphor.' As parents we have to work to keep their hearts soft and seeking.

That is why I am so burdened by the assault from Internet pornography on the lives of our children. Pornography fills them with lies. Because it has such a jolt in the brain, they remember and learn and get seduced into the trap. I have filled the back appendix with many useful resources to help you confront pornography in your family.

We are the generation of parents called by God to deal with this issue of Internet pornography. None of us asked for the beast to come to dinner; but he showed up. We can feed him, put him back in his cage, or we can simply ignore that's he's in the family room playing with our children.

WHERE DO PARENTS BEGIN TO DEAL WITH THE THREAT OF INTERNET PORNOGRAPHY?

- **Start by getting your home clean.** If there is anything in your home that is pornographic; children will find it. It will destroy their respect for you as well as enable their process of addiction.

- **Keep the computer in a central area of the house.** As unsophisticated as this sounds, the computer needs to be in the highest traffic area of the house. Then learn to recognize body language. Hovering over a screen or quickly changing screens when you walk in the room is a little suspicious.

- **Learn to filter.** Filters are not perfect. We still need to be vigilant parents. However, filters are an additional aid to help parents keep a good part of pornography out of our homes. There is an excellent website in the resources hosted by New Life Community Church in Stafford, Virginia with a tremendous amount of information about filters versus Christian servers. Learn to go back into the history of your computer to see where your children have been.

- **Find out who's on your side in the battle.** Most libraries have decided not to filter pornography. At the current time, this tends to work against what we are trying to accomplish as parents. However, parents who truly care and get involved can make powerful inroads at their local libraries. It is by discussing the issues one person at a time that hearts will change. Get involved. Don't be deceived by the idea that filtering is censorship and takes away freedom of speech. When you come to understand the power of addiction, you will understand that unrestricted access to pornography is taking away the freedom of our children. Unrestricted access to pornography will ultimately place them into the bondage of pornography addiction. Sound a little dramatic? Start exploring the information in the resource section on your own. But do it soon, while you can still make a difference in the lives of your children.

- **Use available resources.** A great resource to be aware of is the website www.screenit.com. It will give you information about the sexual content of the movies and videos your children want to see. That website will provide you with current movie reviews as to sexual content, violence, bad attitude, foul language, etc. It will rate the movies in a table format as well as give you a narrative description of the scenes that may be offensive.

ADDICTIONS ALWAYS START BY CREATING A SENSE OF PLEASURE IN THE BRAIN

With all that in mind, let's try to make understanding addictions "user friendly." Remember that the things we become addicted to always start by creating a sense of pleasure in the brain. Your brain learns to enjoy the way something makes you feel. That's the seduction part. Many times children get lured into addictions because they carry a tremendous load of emotional pain from which they seek relief.

Addictions are among the most powerful motivators we can imagine. People are known to abandon the children they love to satisfy an addiction. Addictions are beasts. A great way to explain this to children is the metaphor of the two battling tigers that live within the heart. One vies for true love and the other for sexual pleasure. Who will win? Whichever one you feed!

If you start down the road toward a pornography addiction, the slope gets slippery both quickly and unpredictably. This is where your testimony with youth becomes essential if you are struggling with sexual wholeness. They need to understand from us that this is a human desire common to all of us. There is no sin that is not common to us all. Nobody escapes. We are all sexual beings and will have the same temptations. All of us. Male and female. As parents, we can provide the perspective. We can hopefully ward off years and years of bondage.

In the brain, once the child learns that viewing pornography brings a sense of sexual pleasure the reward pathway gets activated. The primary cravings of the body come from the **'Reward Center.'** Normally the reward center is a blessing. It tells us we're hungry and rewards us with the signal that we are satisfied.

Dopamine is the primary neurotransmitter of pleasure that acts in the reward center. The common denominator of all addictions is a surge of dopamine released into the nucleus accumbens of the mesolimbic dopamine system. We'll just call it the reward pathway. It starts in the midbrain and connects to the thinking brain in the prefrontal cortex.

When addiction starts, we find ourselves seeking out a certain stimulus to create the pleasure feeling that is the reward. Now, addictions are not simple! They are created by a complex interplay of psychosocial, environmental and genetic factors. A basic premise, however, is that something is missing that they are seeking. Ron Hutchcraft states it simply:

> All young people know that there's a relation-

ship missing- someone who is supposed to be there but isn't. They think it's a boyfriend, girlfriend, a best friend, a group of friends, a close family, someone to get married to, a baby. But no earth person can fill the hole in their hearts. It's God that they are missing. [13]

Whatever the complex interplay of factors is for each person, the addiction starts. No one ever intends for it to become an addiction. But over-stimulation of the reward center of the brain creates long-lasting brain changes. This is important to realize. Once the addiction starts, we begin dealing with a brain that starts to change its physical structure. And the process of what is happening in the brain directly parallels what happens in the person's behavior.

A key part of the process of addiction revolves around the changes in the receptors of the brain itself. **Neurons in the addicted brain change their genetic and protein makeup.**

Most of the studies of the molecular basis to the sexual response were done in animals. We understand so far that endorphins released during orgasm stimulate the opioid receptors. [13] These are some of the most potent pleasure chemicals. Opiate like chemicals act indirectly to increase Dopamine release.

Dopamine is the pleasure neurotransmitter. When the neurons of the reward pathway are stimulated, they send connections all over the body to create the sensation of pleasure. These produce a profound sense of euphoria and well being in the person.

THE BODY HAS BUILT IN MECHANISMS TO TRY TO SELF-REGULATE

Our reward system is designed to maintain its balance. It is not designed to be over-stimulated. The body has built in mechanisms to try to self-regulate. If an area of the nervous system is being stimulated more than it is designed to handle, it will either change its number of receptors or its amount of neurotransmitter. In this case we know that the brain down-regulates the number of Dopamine receptors.

This is very interesting. The brain of the person who is becoming addicted is physically changing! It is making less Dopamine receptors.

Unfortunately, less Dopamine receptors mean that it will take more of a stimulus for the body to achieve the same pleasure response. So if the addiction is to a drug, like alcohol, it takes more of the drug to create the same effect. When we are dealing with pornography, we find that the images need to be more graphic.

But the cycle does not stop there. The increased stimulation to the brain will again result in more down-regulation. More Dopamine receptors are pruned from the neurons. And we have now entered the deadly cycle of human addiction. We need more and more to stimulate a brain that is making fewer receptors.

We need to take any possible steps to prevent our children from addictions. They hold us in unbelievable bondage.

We are also beginning to realize that the adolescent brain is uniquely vulnerable to addictions. High stress levels also make us more susceptible to addictions. [14] [15]

The cycle is vicious. Remember that at this point, a person no longer has the same normal brain he knew before the addiction started. This is a great oversimplification of complex chemical and behavioral triggers. However, it is meant to lay a foundation in the understanding that addictions are huge. Addictions motivate us in our behaviors; and chemically they change the brain.

THE WORD OF GOD WORKS WITH TREMENDOUS GRACE

This is the one area where I have seen the Word of God work with tremendous grace. Healing of pornography addictions occurs when one clings to and puts the Word of God into one's struggling neural networks. Key encouraging authors and books in this area are: Mark Laaser in *Faithful and True* and Robert Daniels in *The War Within.*

See if these stages of pornography addiction make sense now that we understand the cycle in the brain.

STAGES OF PORNOGRAPHY ADDICTION

1. Addiction; the desire to keep coming back for pornographic images.
2. Escalation; the need for more explicit, rougher, and more deviant images for the same sexual effect.
3. Desensitization; material once viewed as shocking or taboo is seen as acceptable or commonplace.
4. Acting out; the tendency to perform the behaviors viewed, including exhibitionism, sadistic/masochistic sex, rape or sex with minor children. [16]

The National Coalition for the Protection of Children and Families is a great first resource in the battle with pornography. Its brochure *Tips and Talking Points: An Age Appropriate Guide For Discussing The Harms Of Pornography With Your Family* is an excellent resource for parents to help with discussing the issues of pornography in a sensitive way at different ages. Equipping our children without exposing them to pornographic images remains the target while the brain is developing. Keep them focused on Christ. He heals. As simple as it seems, He is what is missing.

THE POWER OF THE PICTURE: HOW PORNOGRAPHY HARMS

One monograph from the National Coalition described the effects of nonviolent pornography on men. They describe that research conducted by Dolf Zillman and Jennings Bryant on normal adult males exposed to heavy doses of nonviolent adult pornography for 6 weeks had the following results:

1. They developed an increased callousness toward women.

2. They trivialized rape as a criminal offense.

3. They exhibited distorted perceptions about sexuality.

4. They revealed an appetite for more deviant, bizarre, or violent types of pornography.

5. They devalued monogamy and showed lack of confidence in marriage as either a viable or lasting institution.

6. They viewed non-monogamous relationships as moral and natural behavior. [17]

The National Institute on Media and the Family also has excellent resources to help with overall Internet safety. They suggest that children be taught some basic cyber-smarts like never giving identifying information out on-line and staying out of chat rooms. Parents are lagging a little behind in understanding the risks of the Internet. Last year statistics revealed that,

In regard to the internet, 67% of parents think the

> most important role of parents is as a guide to the good content; 24% think the most important role of parents is as a watchdog; 60% of parents whose children use the internet say they restrict their children's use in some ways. Among those who restrict the amount of time children can spend online, 12% restrict chat room use or instant messaging. [18]

There are several other resources that are helpful in dealing with the sexuality of your child and risk of pornography addiction. Joshua Harris has a 3-video series that deals with the concept of "True Love." [19] The video on Purity in his series helps young women understand that the way they choose to dress can truly lead a Christian brother into lust. It is convicting! Also, PBS Frontline produced *The Lost Children of Rockdale County*. [20] It is an expository story on the 1999 syphilis epidemic in Suburban Atlanta. It is a movingly accurate depiction of the Christian and non-Christian youth culture in terms of sexuality.

Satan battles ferociously because human sexuality is a tremendous gift. Christian parents have to enter this battle fully recognizing that Satan has already been defeated. We have to humbly ask Jesus Christ where He wants us in this battle. We have to resist the overwhelming urge to bury our head in the sand or get back on the fence. Jesus Christ chose each of us (and our children) to be here at this moment in the battle for human sexuality. He will lead us if we will seek His heart. The beast does not have permission to devour our children!

CHAPTER 14

"WHOEVER TELLS the STORIES, DEFINES the CULTURE"

Dr. David Walsh, president of the National Institute on Media and the Family made the statement that "Whoever tells the stories defines the culture." [1] It is profound in many ways and pertinent to our concluding thoughts.

We are a culture that passes down our values through our story telling. The authors of *The Sacred Romance* describe that; "the deepest convictions of our heart are formed by stories and reside there in the images and emotions of story." [2] The Jewish culture has consistently passed down stories and heritage through the meaning behind their religious holidays.

Many of us, however, are living separated from our family of origin. We don't have a feeling for our own unique cultural stories. They have been replaced by the stories of larger culture. David Walsh writes:

> While the important role of storytelling has remained constant for thousands of years, a monumental change has happened in the past fifty years. Since World War II we have delegated an ever larger portion of the story-

> telling function to mass media, especially television. This has changed who tells the stories and how they are told. [3]

What is our story? The Sacred Romance reveals that:

> Through baseball and politics and music and sex and even church, we are searching desperately for a larger story in which to live and find our role. All of these smaller stories offer a taste of meaning, adventure, or connectedness. But, none of them offer the real thing; they aren't large enough. Our loss of confidence in a larger story is the reason we demand immediate gratification. We need a sense of being alive now, for now is all we have. Without a past that was planned for us; and a future that waits for us, we are trapped in the present. There's not enough room for our souls in the present. [4]

Alexander Solzhenitsyn commented, "Man has forgotten God, that is why this has happened." [5]

CHILDREN NEED STORIES TO HELP FORM THEIR VALUES AND THEIR VIEW OF THE WORLD

Children need stories. They need to understand their reason for existence. They learn to see God through our stories of personal faith, through reading letters from the missionaries we support, and through character stories. They need multiple stories to form their values and their view of the world. They need word-pictures, like the ones we painted earlier in this book, to bring structure to their tough decisions.

Tell it to your children, and let your children tell it to their children, and their children to the next generation.
Joel 1:3

This needs to raise concerns for us as parents. Are we content to give responsibility for the storytelling to our TV and moviemakers? What exactly are the values they will be teaching our children? We are in the throws of a billion-dollar movie-making industry here in the United States. Unfortunately our moviemakers export their movie extravaganzas around the globe. The rest of the world has noticed and has asked for help.

In 1946 the United States formally joined the United Nations Educational, Scientific, and Cultural Organization (UNESCO).[6] In 1998, UNESCO published *Children and Media Violence: A Yearbook from UNESCO International Clearinghouse on Children and Violence on the Screen.* It reviews studies of media violence from 25 countries and pleads concern about 'the global aggressive culture' being created by the exportation of US violent TV, films, and video games." [7] A large part of the world is asking us to stop the exportation of violent programming. They are trying to raise healthy children the same as we are. Nowhere in the world does the human child thrive under a barrage of violent programming!

The difference is that we are providing the funds for American moviemakers to host their assault on children around the world. We buy the movies. We attend the movies or allow our children to see those films with money that God has trusted us to allocate for His story. We are supposed to be the watchmen on the walls of world freedom and yet we are contributing to its violence.

In 1963, President John F. Kennedy said,

> We in this country, in this generation, are- by destiny rather than choice- the watchmen on the walls of world freedom. We ask, therefore, that we may be worthy of our power and responsibility, that we may exercise our strength with wisdom and restraint, and that we may achieve for our time the ancient vision of peace on earth, goodwill toward men. That must always be our goal...For as was written long ago, 'Except the Lord keep the city, the watchman waketh but in vain.' [8]

OUR NEW CULTURAL ELITES HAVE DIFFERENT VALUES THAN THE GENERAL PUBLIC

Interesting research shows that the values of our culturally elite, those who are in positions of power to pass down our culture through their stories, actually do not have values that represent the general public. While this may be obvious by the type of media that is generated by our moviemakers, I think the magnitude of the differences may surprise you.

The most interesting study was done for the National Institute for Healthcare Research "Religion Among American Elites, with Comparisons to the General Public." [9] Parts of the research were published in *American Elites* by Lerner, Nagai and Rothman. [10] In this study, data was collected by personal interviews of 1,800 elites from 1979-1986 by Lichter and Rothman. Elites in the area of culture are considered those people who disseminate knowledge and culture; i.e. they are the people who tell the stories. This included print and TV leading journalists, scientists, intellectuals, religious leaders, TV writers, directors, and producers, leading movie writers, directors and producers.

Our American culture is now being defined by the

stories of our moviemakers that largely do not believe that God exists. Among the conclusions of the study the authors noted that:

> Those who believe in traditional social morality tend to be quite religious and believe that religion has an important role to play in society; those who do not believe are far less religious and tend to want to reduce or minimize the influence of religion on society. [11]

WHO ARE THE STORYTELLERS? WHAT ARE THEIR VALUES? A SUMMARY OF THE STUDY OF CULTURAL 'ELITES'

1. "Elites" are defined as those who are in positions of power to pass down our culture through their stories such as moviemakers, people within the media, scientists and political leaders.

2. As they became adults, many more elite group members shifted away from religious affiliation than did members of the general public.

3. Proportionately more elites shifted to having no religious affiliation.

4. Among those cultural elites with careers found in the media and the intellectual community;
40-50% have no religious affiliation.
50% of media elite
54.9% of moviemakers
41.3% of TV makers
41% of the public interest groups have no

religious preference).
This is in marked contrast to other leaders where only
5.3% of labor leaders
7.9% of military officers
13.2% of business leaders
15.9% of judges give "none" as their religious preference.

5. Among the general public, 64.4% of the American public are certain that God exists, and only 6.1% don't believe in God or believe that there is no way to find out if God exists or not.

6. Together, these two studies comparing the general public and the culturally elite support the view that elites are less religious than the American public, at least as far as religious affiliation and belief in God are concerned. [12]

Can we afford to allow our moviemakers to tell a counterfeit story to our children? The authors of *The Sacred Romance* captured the essence of the bigger story:

> Could it be that our lives actually make sense, every part- the good and the bad? Those deep yearnings that catch us by surprise when we hear a certain song on the radio, or watch our children when they aren't aware of being watched, are telling us something that is truer about life than the Message of the Arrows. It seems too good to be true, which ought to raise even deeper suspicions that it is true. As Chesterton recounts in "Orthodoxy", he 'had always believed that the world involved magic: now I thought perhaps it involved a magician...I had always felt life first as a story; and if there is a story there is a storyteller. [13]

Our children need to hear the real story. They need to meet Jesus Christ, the Greatest Story Teller.

> Satan is constantly at work deconstructing the Sacred Romance in our heart so that he may more easily seduce us to the smaller stories he is telling. Given all this, it becomes crucial that we become a generation of storytellers who are both recapturing the glory and joy of the Sacred Romance even as we tell each other our particular stories, so that we can help each other, through God's Spirit, see his plan of redemption at work in us. [14]

WE HAVE TO TELL OUR STORIES TO OUR CHILDREN; AND THEN WE HAVE TO TELL OUR STORY TO A BIGGER CULTURE

We have to tell our stories. We have to tell our stories to our children, and then we have to tell our story to a bigger culture. We have to walk with the wounded and be willing to speak of a love that is transcendent and real. We have to tell our stories. We have to tell people that what they are really looking for can be found in Jesus Christ. He is the only person that can fill that hole in their heart. We have to tell our stories. We have to bring hope to the wounded and tell them there is healing; we have walked that path already. They can trust our story because we have walked the same road and have found His healing. We have to tell our stories. We have to tell people that there are answers to the pain and chaos in the lives of their children.

Given all this, it becomes crucial that we become a generation of storytellers who are both recapturing the glory and joy of the

---

Sacred Romance even as we tell each other our particular stories. [15]

It is worth repeating Ron Hutchcraft's insight: "Every teenager understands, values, and longs for relationships. All young people know there's a relationship missing- someone who is supposed to be there- but isn't. They think it's a boyfriend, girlfriend, a best friend, a group of friends, a close family, someone to get married to, a baby. But no earth person can fill the hole in their hearts. It's God that they are missing." [16] Tell them the Bigger Story.

Many famous people have tried to rekindle the fire and tell us the same thing. What is it that keeps us lulled to sleep? The time to wake up is now.

Mother Teresa of Calcutta said, "I see Jesus in every human being. I say to myself, this is hungry Jesus, I must feed him. This is sick Jesus. This one has leprosy or gangrene; I must wash him and tend to him. I serve because I love Jesus." [17]

Back in the chaotic times of the 1860's, George Hay Stuart (President of the Christian Commission during the Civil War) stated, "Brethren, buckle on your armor for a great conflict; buckle it on for giving the glorious Gospel of the Son of God to the millions of the earth who are perishing for lack of knowledge." [18]

Pope John Paul carries the same burdened heart as many of us! He spoke these words to a group of American youth in 1993:

> A 'culture of death' seeks to impose itself on our desire to live, and live to the full...In our own century, as at no other time in history, the 'culture of death' has assumed a social and institutional form of legality to justify the most horrible crimes against humanity....The family especially is under attack. And, the sacred

> character of Human Life is denied... Do not be afraid to go out on the streets and into public places... This is no time to be ashamed of the Gospel. It is time to preach it from the rooftops.... You must feel the full urgency of the task. Woe to you if you do not succeed in defending life. The church needs your energies, your enthusiasm, your youthful ideas, in order to make the Gospel of Life penetrate the fabric of society, transforming people's hearts and the structures of society in order to create a civilization of true justice and love. [19]

Remember our vision of the soda can in the beginning? 1John 4:4 "the one who is in you is greater than the one who is in the world." Consider the encouragement of Ben Franklin in 1778 when he said, "Whoever shall introduce into public affairs the principles of primitive Christianity will change the face of the world." [20]

We only need to tell our story to one person at a time and work within our circle of influence. We are designed to be of service. God designed cells for empathy into the brain as we were still growing inside the uterus! They are essential. Schuyler Colfax (Vice-president under Ulysses S. Grant) stated;

> Man derives his greatest happiness not by that which he does for himself, but by what he accomplishes for others. This is a sad world at best- a world of sorrow, of suffering, of injustice, and falsification; men stab those whom they hate with the stiletto of slander, but it is for the followers of our Lord to improve it, and to make it more as Christ would have it. The most precious crown of fame that a

> human being can ask is to kneel at the bar of God and hear the beautiful words, "Well done, good and faithful servant." [21]

How would our Lord have it? Be reminded that He works through us here. Our Lord will have whatever we will give him through our obedience.

"And God placed all things under his feet and appointed him to be head over everything for the church, which is his body, the fullness of him who fills everything in every way."
Ephesians 1:22

He needs to use us! We are his body here on earth. He has prepared us for his works of service to a world that is asking for his love. He will use us to bring his healing to a wounded world. Ephesians 4:12-13, "to prepare God's people for works of service, so that the body of Christ may be built up until we all reach unity in the faith and in the knowledge of the Son of God and become mature, attaining the full measure of the fullness of Christ."

This is the key for us as parents. Once we mature in Christ, the world cannot affect us. And, therefore, we are also more able to provide that buffer for our children.

We will no longer be infants, tossed back and forth by the waves, and blown here and there by every wind of teaching and by the cunning and craftiness of men in their deceitful scheming. Instead, speaking the truth in love, we will in all things grow up into him who is the Head, that is, Christ. From him the whole body, joined and held together by every supporting ligament, grows and builds itself up in love, as each part does its work.
Ephesians 4:14-16

It's time to take off the bubble wrap. While we look at the fierce changes our culture is going through, we recoil in fear. We want to shelter our children from the strong force of hate and violence engulfing this generation. Matthew 5:14 says "You are the light of the world. A city on a hill cannot be hidden." We possess the knowledge that our dying world needs. We can't sleep through the battle!

THE WORLD HAS REWRITTEN GOD'S STORY

A few months ago I served as a panelist at a Domestic Violence Awareness event. As I sat on the stage and listened to the questions and comments from the people in the auditorium, I was struck by the incredible amount of pain that still filled the lives of the 'survivors'. In my heart, I wept to even imagine the amount of ridicule and abuse they had endured in their homes. I wept to imagine the amount of pain that was required to close down their hearts and leave them so wounded. These were beautiful incredible women with very deep wounds.

Then I thought of the man that had become her abuser. This man also had a life that started as a beautiful little boy for which God had great plans. He was also lovingly created with tenderness. Yet, his 'script' was rewritten by the violence in his home when he grew up. His 'script' was rewritten so that it didn't provide caring adults that could recognize his emotional needs. Tough boys don't need hugs. How many times had he heard that until his neural networks were trained to believe it. His 'script' was rewritten by maltreatment. This man was once a beautiful little boy.

Yes God may still work His plan for him but it probably won't come from his parents; unless we can bring God's love into that struggling home. Quite probably, God will use Mrs. Jones, his teacher. She feels a little helpless because she can't change his home, but she slips a little extra food to him everyday because he comes to school hungry. He knows she cares in a funny kind of way. And God will use Mr. Miner. He's retired now. He putters in his yard a lot and encourages this little boy to learn about plants and digging in the earth.

But, do you know whom God will use the most? Do you know who will make the biggest difference? It will be your son! Because you have taught him to care, your son will be the one who throws the football to that little boy every day at recess and invites him to be part of the game.

Do you remember the research about peers? "...children's social adjustment may depend on the degree to which they obtain helpful, caring responses from peers, in addition to the degree to which they successfully avoid aggressive overtures." [22] Our children will make a difference.

I remember reading a story about Virgil Gulker who founded an organization called *Kids Hope USA*. In his program, he takes volunteers from neighborhood churches and pairs them with an at risk student to spend one single hour a week with him or her at school, "reading, doodling, working math problems, shooting hoops or just listening. The aim is to become the child's friend, a dependable source of encouragement and love. What has stunned not only teachers and administrators, but Gulker himself, is the payoff from such a meager investment. Teachers consistently reported significant improvements in attendance, truancy and academic achievement." [23]

It takes such a meager little amount of our time to make a huge difference in the lives Jesus Christ is trying to guide back on track. We have the deep redeeming love of Jesus Christ to offer a world that is perishing. It takes so little to make a real difference. Most of the time, we don't even have to leave our circle of influence to make a difference. We can make a huge difference in our family or extended family. We can notice the children that are hurting in our neighborhood and at our kid's school. We can reach out to children at church. If we decide to enter bigger volunteer situations, it will only bless our children to take them with us. Let them understand the joy that comes from giving and doing for other people. Let them see ways Christ can use them at every phase of their life. Learn to role model service. It will bless your children as well as bring Christ's healing to the wounded.

---

1 Peter 3:15 tells us to tell our stories: "But in your hearts set apart Christ as Lord. Always be prepared to give an answer to everyone who asks you to give the reason for the hope that you have. But do this with gentleness and respect."

Colossians 3:12-13 says, "Therefore as God's chosen people, holy and dearly loved, clothe yourselves with compassion, kindness, humility, gentleness and patience. Bear with each other and forgive whatever grievances you may have against one another. Forgive as the Lord forgave you."

We have to let God use us! Put aside the busyness and get back into real relationships with people.

The only way to help end the pain is to walk alongside the wounded. Be a consistent loving person. Remember that their scripts have been rewritten for them by their world. It will take time for them to learn to trust again. If you decide to walk with a wounded heart, please make a commitment that you will not become part of their wounding. They will need help in understanding that there truly is a God who loves them, and He has a wonderful plan for them. They will need to see God in you or in your child. They will have to learn to trust for perhaps the first time. Be patient.

1 Peter 3:15 says, "But in your hearts set apart Christ as Lord. Always be prepared to give an answer to everyone who asks you to give the reason for the hope that you have. But do this with gentleness and respect." Respect is the key. Accept silence. Don't be overzealous. Even trained counselors are careful to invite the release of hidden pain in only very small pieces. Avoid judgements. "Nonjudgmental people are not soft on evil, they are soft on people due to an awareness of their own frailties and personal potential for failure." [24]

Remember that true Christian love is not sentiment. It is based in something so much bigger. It is based on solid knowledge of the character of God. Christian love doesn't come from us. It comes from the Holy Spirit moving through us to love those that have been lost. God merely uses us as his vessel.

1 Corinthians 13:7 says that love, "always protects, always trusts, always hopes and always perseveres." We are never called to expose the faults of the wounded. They are already struggling with a huge amount of shame they did not deserve. Rather, remember that emotional support alone will bring them freshness to life. Just walking alongside them will start to ease the pain. Only Jesus Christ will bring healing.

Our testimony is very powerful.
We don't have to understand all of divine revelation to tell our story. We just have to tell people the change that Jesus made in our lives.

Be aware of this relentless increase we are all experiencing in the rate of change. Recognize it for what it is and then cling to our God who is unchanging. Pay attention to the warning signs of over-commitment. Pray more and ask God to bring you an inner peace when an involvement is one to which He is calling you. Satan would love to keep your line busy when God calls. Stay close to God. If he's on the throne of your heart it will be easier to recognize false motives for the trap of over-involvement. Keep the Sabbath. We have seen through this entire book that we need the rest the Sabbath offers for our physical bodies to lower our stress hormones. We have seen through this book that we need that time to renew our minds and break strongholds that are developing in our thought processes. We need to do this on a regular basis. There is very real spiritual warfare! In order to keep our neural networks healthy and filled with the truth we need the continual renewing presence of God. Remember that if we intend to be salt and light; our batteries need to stay charged!

Focus on the Joy! Have you heard J.O.Y stand for Jesus: Others: Yourself? Joy comes from the obedience of Jeremiah 1:7-8: "But the Lord said to me, 'Do not say, 'I am only a child'. You must go to everyone I send you to and say whatever I command you. Do not be afraid of them, for I am with you and will rescue you,' declares the Lord."

The final stanza of *The Journey* by Tom Krause reads:

> "And when your life's voyage is over,
> When your sun starts to set in the sea,
> Pass on to the next generation,
> The joy that the journey can be." [25]

Joel 1:3 "Tell it to your children, and let your children tell it to their children, and their children to the next generation."
Start now passing down an incredible heritage filled with the life and love from Jesus Christ.

Jesus has already accomplished his redemptive

work. The Holy Spirit will work in the hearts that are opened. The hard work has already been done. Satan is already defeated. Only we can give him back power in our lives. Please understand, we just have to tell our stories and give our testimony. It is that simple. We don't have to be spiritual scholars. God has raised up an army of people trained to take over for you once you have worked to soften a heart.

Revelation 12:10-11 says, "Now have come the salvation and the power and the Kingdom of God, and the authority of his Christ.
For the accuser of our brothers, who accuses them before our God day and night,
has been hurled down.
They overcame him by the blood of the Lamb and by the word of their testimony."

Our testimony is very powerful. We don't have to understand all of divine revelation to tell our story. We just have to tell people the change that Jesus made in our lives.

John 4:39 "Many of the Samaritans from that town believed in him because of the woman's testimony, 'He told me everything I ever did.'"

During the healing at the pool, the invalid simply said, "The man who make me well said to me, 'Pick up your mat and walk.' "John 5:11

Matthew 9:30-31 "and their sight was restored. Jesus warned them sternly, 'See that no one knows about this.' But they went out and spread the news about him all over that region."

We just have to tell our story. It doesn't need frills or bells or whistles. It just needs to be the truth.

And what about our children?

There are many resources to help equip your child with a heart that loves Jesus and hands that are ready. In regards to public schools, the schools may not prevent our children from expressing their personal religious beliefs just because they speak about Jesus. Students are allowed to pray in a non-disruptive manner during the school day when they aren't involved in their studies. The U.S. Department of Education has available *The Parents Guide to Religion in the Public Schools.* [26] Gateways to Better Education has Teacher-Reacher packets to help you reach out in love to your child's teacher. Their ministry is meant to bring support to Christian public school families. [27]

Let's conclude simply with one final thought from Beth Moore. She summarizes the whole reason for this book:

I challenge you to grasp this truth: we will never be successful as parents to our children until we are successful at being children to our Heavenly Father. [28]

May He hold you close to His heart.
May you be blessed on your journey.

References

Introduction

1. Dr. Michael Phelps, Norton Simon Professor Chair, Department of Molecular and Medical Pharmacology; Associate Director, Laboratory of Structural Biology and Molecular Biology, Chief Division of Nuclear Medicine, UCLA, Personal Communication.

Chapter 1

1. Bushman, Brad J.; Anderson, Craig. "Media Violence and the American Public: Scientific Facts Versus Media Misinformation," *American Psychologist* June/July 2001, p. 477-489.
2. Ellison, Craig. "Should self-esteem be esteemed?" *Christian Counseling Today*; 9:1 (2000), p. 18.
3. Hutchcraft, Ron. *The Battle For a Generation* (Moody Press: Chicago, 1996), p. 171.
4. Hutchcraft, p. 172.
5. Marshall, Peter. From Federer, William J. *America's God and Country Encyclopedia of Quotations* (St. Louis: Amerisearch, Inc., 2000), p. 418.
6. Henry, Patrick. From Federer, p. 290.

Chapter 2

1. Barton, David. "The shifting paradigm: Where will it end? The law and evolution." *The Wallbuilder Report* (1994; Fall), p. 2.
2. Darwin, Charles From Federer, William J. *America's God and Country: Encyclopedia of Quotations* (St. Louis: Amerisearch, Inc., 2000), p. 199.

3. Darwin, Charles From Federer, p. 199.
4. Swenson, Richard M.D. *Margin: Restoring Emotional, Physical, Financial & Time Reserves to Overloaded Lives* (Colorado Springs: NavPress, 1992), p. 26.
5. Elkind, David From Swenson, p. 62.
6. Swenson, Appendix pp. 247-254.
7. Bushman, Brad J.; Anderson, Craig. "Media Violence and the American Public: Scientific Facts Versus Media Misinformation," *American Psychologist* (June/July 2001), p. 478.
8. Lincoln, Abraham, From Federer, p. 380.
9. Carver, George Washington, From Federer, p. 96.
10. Wilson, Woodrow, From Federer, p. 698.
11. Coolidge, Calvin, From Federer, p. 181.
12. *Compton's Interactive Encyclopedia CD ROM* (Compton's Home Library: The Learning Company, 1998) pp. "Thomas Aquinas."
13. Schaeffer, Francis. *How Should We Then Live? The Rise and Decline of Western Thought and Culture* (Wheaton; Crossway Books,1976), p. 82.
14. Compton's, pp. "Thomas Aquinas."
15. Compton's, pp. "Thomas Aquinas."
16. Compton's, pp. "Renaissance."
17. Compton's, pp. "Reformation."
18. Schaeffer, p. 81.
19. Schaeffer, p. 81.
20. Schaeffer, p. 82.
21. Compton's, pp. "Age of Enlightenment."
22. McDowell, Josh and Hostetler, Bob, *Right from Wrong* (Dallas: Word Publishing, 1994), p. 30.
23. Compton's, pp. "Reformation."
24. Compton's, pp. "Romanticism."
25. Compton's, pp. "Romanticism."
26. Compton's, pp. "Romanticism."
27. Darwin, Charles, In Barton, David. "The shifting paradigm: Where will it end? The law and evolution." *The Wallbuilder Report* (1994; Fall), p. 2.

28. Barton, David. "The shifting paradigm: Where will it end? The law and evolution." *The Wallbuilder Report* (1994;Fall), p. 4.
29. Compton's, pp. "Havelock Ellis."
30. Falk, Andrew, "The Sorry Sanger Saga: A Sexual Crusader Reaps Barrenness," *Family Policy* (Family Research Council: 1999) Vol. 12, No. 1, p. 6.
31. United States Supreme Court (1963) in the case of School District of Abington Township v. Schempp from Fehrer, p. 605.
32. Lee, Cameron. "The postmodern turn in family therapy," *Christian Counseling Today* Vol.9 No.3 (2001), p. 17.
33. Moreland, J.P. "A philosophical review of post modernism for Christian counselors." *Christian Counseling Today* Vol 9 No. 3 (2001), p. 14.
34. McKinley, William. From Fehrer, p 444.
35. Moreland, J.P., p.14.
36. Lincoln, Abraham. From Fehrer, p.576.
37. Stowe, Harriet Beecher, *Uncle Tom's Cabin* (New York: Bantam Books, 1851-1852; Reprint 1981), p. 442.
38. Stowe, p.446.
39. Zacharias, Ravi, *Deliver Us From Evil: Restoring the Souls in a Disintegrating Culture.* (Dallas: Word Publishing, 1996), p. 18.
40. Schaeffer, p. 227.

Chapter 3

1. Pritchard, Thomas C. Ph.D. and Alloway, Kevin D. Ph.D., *Medical Neuroscience* (Madison, Connecticut: Fence Creek Publishing, 1999), pp.32-35.
2. Pritchard and Alloway; p.33-34.
3. Pritchard and Alloway; p.35-36.
4. Pritchard and Alloway; p.33.

5. Pritchard and Alloway; p.55-57.
6. Healy, Jane. *Endangered Minds* (New York: Touchstone, 1990), p.56.
7. McNaughton, Bruce in Jensen, Eric, *Teaching with the Brain in Mind* (Alexandria: ASCD Publication, 1998), p.25.
8. www.PBS.org in website text for *The Secret Life of the Brain* (2002).
9. Healy, *Endangered Minds*, p. 15.
10. Healy, Jane, *Your Child's Growing Mind* (New York: Doubleday, 1994), p.19.
11. Jensen, Eric, *Teaching with the Brain in Mind* (Alexandria: ASCD Publication, 1998) p. 15.
12. Healy, *Your Child's Growing Mind*, p. 38.
13. Healy, *Endangered Minds*, pp. 79-80.
14. Jensen, p. 21.
15. Damasio, Antonio, *Descartes' Error: Emotion Reason and the Human Brain* (New York: Avon Books, 1994), p.76.
16. Raleigh, Michael, In Damasio, pp. 76-77.
17. Patrick, Christopher T., Cuthbert, Bruce N., and Lang, Peter J., "Emotion in the Criminal Psychopath: Fear Image Processing," *Journal of Abnormal Psychology*, Vol. 103. No. 3 (1994), pp. 523-534.
18. Kotulak, Ronald, *Inside the Brain: Revolutionary Discoveries of How the Mind Works* (Kansas City: Andrews McMeel Publishing, 1997), pp. 87-94.
19. Chugani, Harry T. M.D., "A Critical Period of Brain Development: Studies of Cerebral Glucose Utilization with PET, "*Preventative Medicine*, Vol. 2 (1998), p.186.
20. Larsen, Earnie, Personal Communication, E. Larsen Enterprises, Inc. 7549 Douglas Drive N. Suite 2; Brooklyn Park, MN 55443 or www.earnie.com.
21. Healy, *Your Child's Growing Mind*, pp. 104-105.

22. Salovey, Peter and Mayer, John D., "Emotional Intelligence," *Imagination, Cognition and Personality*, Vol. 9 No. 3 (1989-90), pp. 185-211.
23. Goleman, Daniel, *Emotional Intelligence* (New York: Bantam Books, 1997), p.100 and pp. 116-117.

Chapter 4

1. "Media Wise Curriculum," National Institute on Media and the Family, www.mediafamily.org or 888-672-5437.
2. DeGaetano, Gloria, "Grow Smart Brains Toolkit," *www.growsmartbrains.com*
3. Walsh, David Ph.D. Teaching Seminar in South Washington County (2000) on Media Wise Curriculum.
4. Healy, Jane, *Your Child's Growing Mind* (New York: Doubleday, 1994), p. 100.
5. Jensen, Eric, *Teaching with the Brain in Mind* (Alexandria: ASCD Publication, 1998), p. 22.
6. Jensen, p. 22.
7. Walsh, David, *Jolts and Tricks* Video Format for the Media Wise Curriculum, (National Institute on Media and the Family).
8. Walsh, David, "Seven Building Blocks for School Success" in the Media Wise Curriculum, 888-672-5437.
9. Healy, Jane. *Endangered Minds* (New York: Touchstone, 1990), p. 201
10. DeGaetano, *Grow Smart Brains Toolkit.*
11. Healy, *Endangered Minds*, p. 201.
12. Healy, *Endangered Minds*, p. 199.
13. Healy, *Endangered Minds*, p. 200.
14. Healy, *Endangered Minds*, p. 198.
15. Healy, *Endangered Minds*, p. 199.
16. Kupchella, Rick, in *Plugged In*, National Institute on Media and the Family. www.mediafamily.org

17. Moore, Beth, *Living Beyond Yourself: Exploring the Fruit of the Spirit* (Nashville: Lifeway Press, 1998), p. 187.
18. McDowell, Josh and Hostetler, *Right from Wrong* (Dallas: Word Publishing, 1994), p. 81.
19. McDowell, p. 82.
20. McDowell, p. 82.
21. *Webster's Universal College Dictionary*. (New York: Random House Publishers, 1997), p. 845.
22. Brothers, Leslie, "A biological perspective on empathy," *Am J Psychiatry*, 146(1) (1989), pp. 10-19.
23. Brothers, p. 13.
24. Brothers, p. 15.

Chapter 5

1. Weinberger, Norman M. "The Musical Infant: Studies Show Infants are 'Musical' " *MuSICA Research Notes*, Vol. 1 Issue 1 (Spring 1994), p. 2. www.musica.uci.edu.
2. Weinberger, p. 2.
3. Trehub, S.E., Bull, D. and Thorpe, L.A. "Infants' perception of melodies: The role of melodic contour," *Child Development*, 55 (1984) pp. 821-830 in Weinberger, p.2.
4. Weinberger, Norman M. "The Coloring of Life: Music and Mood," *MuSICA Research Notes*, Vol. 3 (Spring 1996), p. 4.
5. Weinberger, Norman M. "Music and Cognitive Achievement in Children," *MuSICA Research Notes*, Vol. 1 (Fall 1994), p.1.
6. Weinberger, (Fall 1994), p. 2.
7. Garlock, Frank and Woetzel, Kurt, *Music in the Balance* (Greenville, SC: Majesty Music, 1992), p.117.
8. Smith, Kimberly and Smith, Lee, *Oh, Be Careful Little Ears* (Mukilteo, WA: WinePress Publishing, 1997), pp.34-35.

9. Garlock, Frank, *The Language of Music*: Six Part Video Series (Greenville, SC: Majesty Music, 1992).
10. Smith, p. 81.
11. Bartha J. "Making a Hardcore Difference: A Conversation with P.O.D.'s Noah Bernardo," *PluggedIn* 5:7 (2000), p.9.
12. Bloom, Allan, *Closing of the American Mind* (New York: Simon & Schuster, 1987), p.68.
13. Phelps, Michael and Massioto, John, Personal communication. Originally published in *Science* (May 17, 1985).
14. Healy, Jane, *Endangered Minds* (New York: Touchstone, 1990), p.173.
15. Kumar AM, Tims F, Cruess DG et al. "Music therapy increases serum melatonin levels in patients with Alzheimer's disease." *Altern Ther Health Med* Vol. 5(6) (1999),49-57.
16. Gerra G, Zaimovic A, Franchini D et al. "Neuroendocrine responses of healthy volunteers to 'techno-music': relationships with personality traits and emotional state." *Int J Psychophysiol*, Vol 28 (1) (1998), p. 100.
17. Gerra, p. 99.
18. Healy, *Endangered Minds*, p. 175.
19. Gerra, p. 108.
20. Pritchard, Thomas C. Ph.D. and Alloway, Kevin D. Ph.D., *Medical Neuroscience* (Madison, Connecticut: Fence Creek Publishing, 1999), p. 33.
21. Gerra, p. 108.
22. Gerra, p. 103.
23. Gerra, p. 104.
24. Healy, *Endangered Minds*, p. 175.
25. Jensen, Eric, *Teaching with the Brain in Mind* (Alexandria: ASCD Publication, 1998) p. 36.
26. Jensen, p. 87.

27. Jensen, p. 37.
28. Zaccharias, Ravi, Lecture at Bethel College, St. Paul, MN
29. Jensen, p. 37.
30. Jensen, p. 38.
31. Jensen, p. 37.
32. Gerra, p. 100.
33. Took, Kevin J. and Weiss, David S., "The Relationship between Heavy Metal and Rap Music and Adolescent Turmoil: Real or Artifact?" *Adolescence* Vol. 29, No. 115 (Fall 1994), pp. 613-621.
34. Christenson, Peter and Roberts, Donald, *It's Not Only Rock and Roll* (Creskill: Hampton Press, 2001), pp. 102-110.
35. Christenson, p. 102-110.
36. Weinberger, Norman M., "Understanding Music's Emotional Power," *MuSICA Research Notes*, Vol. 5 (Spring 1998), pp.6-7.
37. Smith, p.92.
38. "Noise and Hearing Loss," NIH Consensus Statement Online 1990, Jan. 22-24, 8 (1):1-24
39. www.hearusa.com/audiologist/audiologist_noise_hearing_loss.html
40. www.hearnet.com

Chapter 6

1. Jensen, Eric, *Teaching with the Brain in Mind* (Alexandria: ASCD Publication, 1998), p. 73.
2. McEwen, Bruce S. Ph.D. and Stellar, Elliot Ph.D., "Stress and the Individual: Mechanisms Leading to Disease," *Arch Intern Med* Vol 153 (1993), pp. 2093-2100
Maier, Steven F., Watkins, Linda R. and Fleshner, Monika, "Psychneuroimmunology: The interface Between Behavior, Brain and Immunity," *American Psychologist* Vol. 49 No. 12 (Dec. 1994), pp. 1004-1016.

3. Clinton, Timothy Ed.D., "Anger Management," *Caring For People God's Way BICO 506* (American Association of Christian Counselors).
4. Bland, Jeffrey S. Ph.D., *Nutritional Endocrinology: Breakthrough Approaches for Improving Adrenal and Thyroid Function* (Gig Harbor: Metagenics Educational Programs, 2002), p. 40. www.metagenics.com
5. DeBellis, Michael D., Keshavan, Matcheri S., Clark, Duncan B., et. al. "Developmental Traumatology Part II: Brain Development," *Society of Biological Psychiatry* Vol. 45 (1999), p. 1271.
6. Kotulak, Ronald, *Inside the Brain: Revolutionary Discoveries of How the Mind Works* (Kansan City: Andrews McMeel Publishing, 1997), p.91.
7. *JAMA* Vol. 267 No. 22 (June 10, 1992), p. 3061.
8. Salovey, Peter and Mayer, John D., "Emotional Intelligence," *Imagination, Cognition and Personality*, Vol. 9 No. 3 (1989-90), p. 185.
9. Goleman, Daniel, *Emotional Intelligence* (New York: Bantam Books, 1997), p. 43.
10. Goleman, p. 60.
11. Goleman, p. 60.
12. Christoffel Katherine Kaufer, Study Cutting TV and Video game use can make children less aggressive. *CNN.com* Jan. 14,2001
13. Jensen, p. 19.
14. Goleman, p. 61.
15. Goleman, p. 62.
16. Crick, Nicki R. and Grotpeter, Jennifer K., "Children's treatment by peers: Victims of relational and overt aggression," *Development and Psychopathology* 8 (1996), p. 378.
17. Priolo, Lou, *The Heart of Anger: Practical Help for the Prevention and Cure of Anger in Children* (Amityville, NY : Calvary Press, 1997), pp. 21-22.
18. Priolo, pp. 29-51.

19. Mittleman MA, Maclure M, Sherwood JB et al. "Triggering of acute myocardial infarction onset by episodes of anger. Determinants of Myocardial Infarction Onset Study Investigators." *Circulation* 92(7)(1995),1720-1725.
20. Friedman HS, and Booth-Kewley S., "The "dis-ease-prone personality" : A meta-analytic view of the construct." *Am Psychol* 42(6) (1987), p. 549.
21. Lazar J., "Mind-body medicine in primary care." *Primary Care Clinics in Office Practice* 23(1) (1996), p. 172.

Chapter 7

1. Evans, Tony, *The Battle is the Lord's Video Series* (Moody Press)
2. Moore, Beth, *Living Beyond Yourself: Exploring the Fruit of the Spirit* (Nashville: Lifeway Press, 1998), p. 161.
3. LeDoux JE. "Emotion, memory and the brain," *Sci Am* 270(6) (1994), p. 55.
4. Shames, Richard L. M.D. "Nutritional Management of Stress-Induced Dysfunction," *Applied Nutritional Science Reports* (2002), p. 3.
5. Luther, Martin, In Federer, William J. *America's God and Country: Encyclopedia of Quotations* (St. Louis: Amerisearch, Inc., 2000), p.155.
6. Hutchcraft, Ron, *The Battle for a Generation* (Chicago: Moody Press, 1996), p. 41.

Chapter 8

1. Curtis, Brent and Eldredge, John, *The Sacred Romance: Drawing Closer to the Heart of God* (Nashville: Thomas Nelson, 1997), p. 85.
2. Earnie Larsen, Personal Communication, www.earnie.com
3. Curtis, p. 114-115.

4. LeDoux JE. "Emotion, memory and the brain," *Sci Am* 270(6) (1994), p. 55.
5. LeDoux, p. 55.
6. Salovey, Peter and Mayer, John D., "Emotional Intelligence," *Imagination, Cognition and Personality*, Vol. 9 No. 3 (1989-90), p. 185.

Chapter 9

1. Zaccharias, Ravi, *Deliver Us From Evil: Restoring the Souls in a Disintegrating Culture* (Dallas: Word Publishing, 1996), p. 12.
2. Moore, Beth, *Praying God's Word: Breaking Free from Spiritual Strongholds* (Nashville: Broadman and Holman Publishers, 2000), p. 3.
3. Moore, Beth *Living Beyond Yourself: Exploring the Fruit of the Spirit* (Nashville: Lifeway Press, 1998), p. 160.
4. Curtis, Brent and Eldredge, John, *The Sacred Romance: Drawing Closer to the Heart of God* (Nashville: Thomas Nelson, 1997), p.58.
5. Hutchcraft, Ron, *The Battle for a Generation* (Chicago: Moody Press, 1996), p.11.
6. "The Indispensable Man," Author Unknown.
7. Earnie Larson, Personal Communication, www.earnie.com
8. McDowell, Josh and Hostetler, Bob, *Right from Wrong* (Dallas: Word Publishing, 1994), p. 107-108.

Chapter 10

1. The Promise Bible: New Living Translation, (Wheaton: Tyndale House Publishers, 2001), p.739.

Chapter 11

1. Hutchcraft, Ron, *The Battle for a Generation* (Chicago: Moody Press, 1996), p. 76.
2. *A Call to Prayer: A Season of Harvest.* (Cincinnati: Standard Publishing Company, 1992), p.9.
3. *A Call to Prayer*, p. 17.
4. *A Call to Prayer*, p. 25.
5. *A Call to Prayer*, p. 42.
6. Lee, General Robert E, In Federer, William J. *America's God and Country: Encyclopedia of Quotations* (St. Louis: Amerisearch, Inc., 2000), p. 365.
7. Reagan, Ronald, In Federer, , p. 528.
8. Reagan, Ronald, In Federer, p. 529.
9. Solzhenitsyn, Alexander, In Federer, p. 566.

Chapter 12

1. Moore, Beth *Living Beyond Yourself: Exploring the Fruit of the Spirit* (Nashville: Lifeway Press, 1998), p. 158.
2. Curtis, Brent and Eldredge, John, *The Sacred Romance: Drawing Closer to the Heart of God* (Nashville: Thomas Nelson, 1997), p.120.
3. Hutchcraft, Ron, *The Battle for a Generation* (Chicago: Moody Press, 1996), p. 64.
4. McDowell, Josh and Hostetler, *Right from Wrong* (Dallas: Word Publishing, 1994), p. 21.
5. Moore, Beth, p. 159.
6. Earnie Larsen, Personal Communication, www.earnie.com.

Chapter 13

1. Arterburn, Stephen and Burns, Jim, *Focus on the Family's Parents' Guide to the Top Ten Dangers Teens Face* (Nashville: Word Publishing, 1995), p. 213.

2. Schaeffer, Francis A. *How Should we Then Live? The Rise and Decline of Western Thought and Culture* (Wheaton: Crossway Books, 1976), p. 227.
3. Chambers, Oswald, *My Utmost for His Highest* (Uhrichsville: Barbour Publishing, 1935), p. December 5th.
4. Moore, Beth, *Living Beyond Yourself: Exploring the Fruit of the Spirit* (Nashville: Lifeway Press, 1998), p. 195.
5. Curtis, Brent and Eldredge, John, *The Sacred Romance: Drawing Closer to the Heart of God* (Nashville: Thomas Nelson, 1997), p. 91.
6. Curtis, p. 91.
7. Curtis, p. 91.
8. Arterburn, p. 213.
9. Walsh, David, *Jolts and Tricks Video* National Institute on Media and the Family, www.mediafamily.org.
10. *The Merchants of Cool,* PBS Frontline Video.
11. Hersch, Patricia, *A Tribe Apart* (New York: Ballantine Publishing, 1996)
12. Hutchcraft, Ron, *The Battle for a Generation* (Chicago: Moody Press, 1996), p.80.
13. Pert, Candace B. *Molecules of Emotion: The Science Behind Mind-Body Medicine* (New York: Touchstone, 1997), p.103-104.
14. Piazza, PV, Maccari, S., Deminiere J., et.al "Corticosterone Levels Determine Individual Vulnerability to Amphetamine Self Administration," *Proc.Natl. Acad.Sci.USA* Vol. 88 No. 6 (March 15, 1991), pp. 2088-2092.
15. Marinelli, Michela, Aouizerate, Bruno, Barrot, Michel et.al. "Dopamine-dependent responses to morphine depend on glucocorticoid receptors," *Proc. Natl. Acad. Sci. USA* Vol 95, No. 13 (June 23, 1998), pp 7742-7747.

16. www.enoughisenough.org.
17. Kirk, Jerry, *The Power of the Picture: How Pornography Harms.* Focus on the Family, 1992.
18. Picker, Lauren, "The Web as Homework Helper," *Newsweek*/ Score: Children Online, 2000.
19. Harris, Joshua, *Searching for True Love Videos: Love; Trust; Purity* (Sisters: Multnomah Publishers, 1999), www.multnomahbooks.com
20. *The Lost Children of Rockdale County*, PBS Frontline Video

Chapter 14

1. *Media Wise Newsletter*, National Institute on Media and the Family, Summer 1999, p. 1.
2. Curtis, Brent and Eldredge, John, *The Sacred Romance: Drawing Closer to the Heart of God* (Nashville: Thomas Nelson, 1997), p. 38.
3. Walsh, David, Personal Communication, www.mediafamily.org
4. Curtis, p. 43.
5. Solzhenitsyn, Alexander In Federer, William J. *America's God and Country: Encyclopedia of Quotations* (St. Louis: Amerisearch, Inc., 2000), p. 566.
6. Finnegan, Kathy, *Goals 2000: Restructuring our Schools/ Restructuring Society* (Oklahoma City: Hearthstone Publishing, 1996)
7. DeGaetano, Gloria, *A Grow Smart Brains Tool Kit:* Challenging Media Violence (2000), www.growsmartbrains.com; 206-654-2994.
8. Kennedy, John Fitzgerald, in Federer p. 346.
9. Lerner, Robert Ph.D. "Religion Among American Elites, with Comparisons to the General Public." (1998) excerpted data from *American Elites* (1996), courtesy of the late Dr. Dave Larson at International Center for the Integration of Health and Spirituality.

10. Lerner, Robert, Nagai, Althea K., and Rothman, Stanley, *American Elites* (New Haven: Yale University Press, 1996).
11. Lerner, p.39.
12. Lerner, p.1-42.
13. Curtis, p.45.
14. Curtis, p.114.
15. Curtis, p. 114.
16. Hutchcraft, Ron, *The Battle for a Generation* (Chicago: Moody Press, 1996), p.80.
17. Mother Teresa of Calcutta in Federer p. 584.
18. Stuart, George Hay in Federer p. 577.
19. Pope John Paul II in Federer p. 516-517.
20. Franklin, Benjamin in Federer p. 246.
21. Colfax, Schuyler in Federer p. 110-111.
22. Crick, Nicki R. and Grotpeter, Jennifer K., "Children's treatment by peers: Victims of relational and overt aggression," *Development and Psychopathology* 8 (1996), p.378.
23. Loconte J. "Bullet Proofing our Schools with Faith. The Story of Virgil Gulker of Kids Hope, USA." *Citizen* Vol.14 No.4 (2000):24-25.
24. "Ten Keys to an Intimate Midlife Marriage," Focus on the Family Pamphlet p. 9.
25. Krause, Tom received via email from Villa Maria College Newsletter, Sister Marcella Marie Garus. Villa Vistas 8/2001.
26. www.ed.gov.
27. Buchrer E. "Help Teachers Help Your Kids". *Focus on the Family Magazine*, October:14, 2000 www.gtbe or 888-706-5601.
28. Moore, Beth *Living Beyond Yourself: Exploring the Fruit of the Spirit* (Nashville: Lifeway Press, 1998), p. 134.

RESOURCES

BRAIN DEVELOPMENT AND NEUROSCIENCE INFORMATION

Excellent overviews for parents:

1. Healy, Jane Ph.D. *Endangered Minds.* New York: Touchstone, 1990.
2. Healy, Jane Ph.D. *Your Child's Growing Mind.* New York: Doubleday, 1994.
3. Jensen, Eric. *Teaching With the Brain in Mind.* Alexandria: ASCD Publication, 1998.
4. Goleman, Daniel. *Emotional Intelligence*. New York: Bantam Books, 1997.
5. Kotulak, Ronald. *Inside the Brain: Revolutionary Discoveries of How the Mind Works.* Kansas City: Andrews McMeel Publishing, 1997.

Scientific Overviews:

1. Damasio, Antonio. *Descartes' Error: Emotion Reason and the Human Brain*. New York: Avon Books, 1994.
2. LeDoux, Joseph. *The Emotional Brain: The Mysterious Underpinnings of Emotional Life.* New York: Touchtone, 1996.
3. Pert, Candace B. *Molecules of Emotion*. New York: Touchstone, 1999.
4. Pritchard, Thomas Ph.D. and Alloway, Kevin Ph.D. *Medical Neuroscience*. Madison, CT: Fence Creek Publishing, 1999.
5. Sapolsky, Robert M. Ph.D. *Biology and Human Behavior: The Neurological Origins of Individuality.* Springfield, VA: The Teaching Company, 1996.

TEACHING DISCERNMENT AND SPIRITUAL GUIDANCE

1. Arterburn, Stephen, and Burns, Jim. *Parents Guide to the Top Ten Dangers Teens Face*. Nashville: Word Publishing, 1995.
2. Chapman, Gary. *The Five Love Languages of Teenagers.* Chicago: Northfield Publishers, 2000.
3. Chase, Betty. *Discipline Them: Love Them: Practical Projects for Parents*. Elgin: Cook Publishing, 1982.
4. Dobson, James. *Emotions: Friend or Foe*. Nashville: Word Publishing, 2000.
5. Dubay, Thomas S.M. *The Evidential Power of Beauty: Science and Theology Meet.* San Francisco: Ignatius Press, 1999.
6. *Ethics: An Early American Handbook: A Reprint of an 1890 Original*. Aledo: Wall builder Press.
7. Harris, Joshua. *I Kissed Dating Goodbye.* Sisters: Multonomah Publishers, 1997.
8. Hart, Archibald D. *Stress and Your Child: Know the Signs and Prevent the Harm*. Dallas: Word, 1992.
9. Hovind, Kent. *Dinosaurs/ Creation/ Evolution.* Creation Science Evangelism, 1997. (850)-479-DINO (3466).
10. Ledbetter, J. Otis and Bruner, Kurt. *Your Heritage: How to be Intentional About the Legacy You Leave*. Colorado Springs: Cook Publishing, 1996.
11. McDowell, Josh. *Don't Check Your Brains at the Door*. Dallas: Word Publishing, 1992.
12. McDowell, Josh and Hostetler, Bob. *Right from Wrong.* Dallas: Word Publishing, 1994.
13. McDowell, Josh. *The New Evidence That Demands a Verdict*. Nashville: Thomas Nelson Publishers, 1999.
14. McDowell, Josh and Hostetler, Bob. *Handbook on Counseling Youth.* Dallas: Word Publishing, 1994
15. Richards, Lawrence O. *It Couldn't Just Happen: Fascinating Facts About God's World:* Dallas: Word, 1987.

16. Trent, John; Osborne, Rick; and Bruner, Kurt. *Spiritual Growth of Children.* Wheaton: Tyndale. 2000.
17. Tripp, Tedd. *Shepherding a Child's Heart.* Wapwallopen: Shepherd Press, 1995.
18. *Noah Webster's Advice to the Young and Moral Catechism.* Aledo: Wallbuilders Press, 1993.
19. Wright, H. Norman. *Resilience: Rebounding When Life's Upsets Knock You Down.* Ann Arbor: Servant Publications, 1997.
20. Weidmann, Jim and Bruner, Kurt. *Family Night Tool Chest: Book 1: Introduction to Family Nights.* Colorado Springs: Chariot Victor, 1997.
21. White, Joe and Weidman, Jim. *Spiritual Mentoring of Teens. Wheaton: Tyndale,* 2001.
22. www.mn-apologetics.org
23. www.creationsafaris.com
24. www.heritagebuilders.org
25. www.new-life.net

HANDLING ANGER

1. Anderson, Neil and Miller, Rich. *Getting Anger Under Control.* Eugene: Harvest House, 2002.
2. Priolo, Lou. *The Heart of Anger: Practical Help for the Prevention and Cure of Anger in Children.* Amityville: Calvary Press, 1997.

PRAYER

1. Anderson, Neil T. *Spiritual Protection of Your Children.* Ventura: Regal Publishing, 1996
2. Anderson, Neil T. *Victory over Darkness.* Ventura: Regal Books, 1990.
3. Christenson, Evelyn. *What Happens When We Pray for Our Families.*Wheaton: Victor Books, 1992.
4. Johnson, Kevin. *Pray Hard: Talk to God with Total Confidence; Early Teen Discipleship.* Bloomington: Bethany House, 2001.

5. Maxwell, John. *Partners in Prayer: Support and Strengthen Your Pastor and Church Leaders*. Nashville: Thomas Nelson, 1996.
6. Moore, Beth. *Praying God's Word: Breaking Free from Spiritual Strongholds*. Nashville: Broadman and Holman Publishers, 2000.
7. Omartian, Stormie. *Power of a Praying Parent.* Eugene: Harvest House, 1995.
8. Tirabassi, Becky. *Let Prayer Change Your Life*. Nashville: Thomas Nelson, 1990.
9. *Prayers That Avail Much.* Tulsa: Word Ministries, Harrison House Publishers, 1980.
10. www.praykids.com
11. www.nationaldayofprayer.org

UNDERSTANDING EMOTIONAL WOUNDS

1. Curtis, Brent and Eldredge, John. *The Sacred Romance: Drawing Closer to the Heart of God*. Nashville: Thomas Nelson, 1997.
2. Moore, Beth. *Living Beyond Yourself: Exploring the Fruit of the Spirit.* Nashville: Lifeway, 1998.
3. Thurman, Chris. *The Lies We Believe Workbook*. Nashville: Thomas Nelson, 1995.
4. Peretti, Frank. *The Wounded Spirit*. Nashville: Word Publishing, 2000.
5. www.joycemeyer.org

MUSIC

1. Christenson, Peter and Roberts, Donald. *It's Not Only Rock and Roll.* Creskill: Hampton Press, 2001.
2. Fisher, Tim. *The Battle for Christian Music*. Greenville: Sacred Music Services, 1992.
3. Garlock, Frank and Woetzel, Kurt. *Music in the Balance*. Greenville: Majesty Music, 1992.
4. Smith, Kimberly and Smith, Lee. *Oh, Be Careful Little Ears*. Mukilteo: Winepress Publishing, 1997.

5. Weinberger, Dr. Norman. Music Research Database at www.musica.uci.edu
6. Christian Music Directory www.ccmusic.org/cmd
7. www.pluggedin.org

GAMES

1. *Armor of God Board Game* (Cincinnati: Standard Publishing, 2000), Ages 5 and up.
2. *Bible Challenge Game* (Tallahassee: Bible Challenge Inc, 1984), All ages.
3. *Choose Your Clues: A Guessing Game of Bible People, Places and Things* (Colorado Springs: Chariot Victor, 1999), Ages 8 and up.
4. *Do You Know*? (Colorado Springs: Cook Publishers, 2000) Ages 5 and up.
5. *The Great Adventure Game* (Wheaton: Tyndale, 2001), Ages 6 and up.
6. *The Happy Highway Game* (Appleton: Aid Association for Lutherans), Ages 5 and up.
7. *Larry Burkett's Money Matters: The Christian Financial Concepts Game* (Colorado Springs: Chariot Victor, 1996), Distributed by Rainfall Educational Toys 800-437-4437, Ages 8 and up.
8. *The Life of Christ: A Christian Bible Game* (Memphis:Christian Bible Games, 1998), Ages 9 and up.
9. *Life Stories: Christian Version* (FNDI Limited Partnership, 1992), Distributed by Talicor Inc. 800-433-GAME, Ages 5 and up.
10. *Money Matters for Kids* (Colorado Springs: Chariot Victor, 1998), Distributed by Rainfall Toys, Ages 5-10.
11. *The New Kids Choices* (Colorado Springs: Chariot Victor, 1996), Distributed by Rainfall Toys, Ages 6-12.
12. *The New Teen Choices* (Colorado Springs: Chariot Victor, 1996), Distributed by Rainfall Toys, Ages 12-18.

TV AND MEDIA

1. National Institute on Media and the Family; Free resources on their website www.mediafamily.org 888-672-5437.
2. Walsh, David Ph.D. *Dr. Dave's Cyberhood: Making Media Choices That Create a healthy Electronic Environment for your Kids.* New York: Simon and Schuster, 2001.
3. www.screenit.com. An excellent review of the content of past and current movies and videos.
4. Center for Media Literacy 310-559-2944.
5. National Coalition on Television Violence 810-489-3177.
6. Waliszewski, Bob and Melchizedek, Jerry. *Bringing out the Worst in Us: The Frightening Truth about Violence, the Media and Our Youth.* (Colorado Springs: Focus on the Family, 1995).
7. www.growsmartbrains.com.

OVERVIEW OF THE CHANGES IN SOCIETY

1. Finnegan, Kathy. *Goals 2000: Restructuring our Schools/ Restructuring Society*. Oklahoma City: Hearthstone Publishing, 1996.
2. Hutchcraft, Ron. *The Battle For a Generation.* Chicago, Moody, 1996
3. LaHaye, Tim and Noebel, David. *Mind Siege.* Nashville, Word, 2000.
4. Lerner, Robert, Nagai, Althea K., and Rothman, Stanley. *American Elites*. New Haven: Yale University Press, 1996.
5. Schaeffer, Francis. *How Should We Then Live? The Rise and Decline of Western Thought.* Wheaton: Crossway Books, 1976.
6. Swenson, Richard, M.D. *Margin: Restoring Emotional, Physical, Financial and Time Reserves to Overloaded Lives. Colorado Springs: NavPress, 1992.*

7. Zaccharias, Ravi. *Deliver Us From Evil: Restoring the Souls in a Disintegrating Culture*. Dallas: Word Publishing, 1996.

VIDEOS

1. *Searching for True Love*; Joshua Harris (Sisters: Multnomah Publishers, 1999); www.multnomah books.com.
2. *The Tangled Web: The War Against Pornography* (National Coalition for the Protection of Children and Families) 513-521-6227.
3. *Pornography: Addictive, Progressive and Deadly: Life on the Edge* (Focus on the Family; Word Publishing: 1994).
1. *Music to Die For: Is Today's Music Killing Our Kids?* Phil Chalmers (Cleveland: American Portrait Films), www.chalmersmusic.com (800) 974-7938.
2. *Jolts & Tricks; Unplug Your Kids; and Plugged In*. MediaWise Curriculum; National Institute on Media and the Family, www.mediafamily.org.
3. *Excess Access: Pornography, Children and the American Library Association*. www.afa.net; 601-844-5036.
4. *Mind over Media: The Power of Making Sound Entertainment Choices* (Focus on the Family: Life on the Edge Curriculum, 2001).
5. *The Lost Children of Rockdale County.* PBS Frontline 1999 www.pbs.org. 800-645-4727 or www.shopPBS.com.
6. *Sex and Young America: The Real Deal.* (National Coalition for the Protection of Children and Families, 2001).
7. *The Merchants of Cool*. PBS Frontline, www.shopPBS.com,1999. Discusses the marketing strategies of MTV and Madison Avenue.
8. *The Language of Music: A Unique Series of Biblical Principles illustrating music and its message.* Dr. Frank Garlock: Majesty Music, 1992.

PORNOGRAPHY

1. *Final Report of the Attorney General's Commission on Pornography.* Nashville: Rutledge Hill Press, 1986.
2. National Coalition for the Protection of Children and Families. www.nationalcoalition.org 800-583-2964 For free materials email ncpcf@eos.net.
3. National Law Center for Children and Families. www.nationallawcenter.org.
4. Citizens for Community Values. www.ccv.org 513-733-5775.
5. National Council on Sexual Addiction and Compulsivity www.ncsac.org. 770-989-9754.

INTERNET PORNOGRAPHY AND YOUR LIBRARY

1. *Making Your Library Family-Friendly: A Guide to Involvement in Your Local Public Library.* (Family Research Council, 2000). www.frc.org. 800-225-4008.

INTERNET SAFETY

1. *Child Safety on the Information Highway.* National Center for Missing and Exploited Children. www.missingkids.org.
2. *Teen Safety on the Information Highway.* www.missingkids.org.
3. *A Parents Guide to Internet Safety*. Free download from the FBI website at www.fbi.gov.
4. *Web smart kids: A Parents Guide to Media Literacy on the Internet*. www.websmartkids.org.
5. Advice for protecting kids on the Internet; www.kidshield.com.
6. Internet Advice; www.getnetwise.org.
7. To report pornographic sites; www.netscrubber.com.

8. www.filterreview.com. Reviews different internet filters.
9. Britton, Sachary. *Safety Net: Guiding and Guarding Your Children on the Internet.* Harvard House Publishers, 1998.
10. Schultze, Quentin. *Internet for Christians: Everything You Need to Start Cruising the Net Today.* Gospel Communications Network, 1996. 800-253-0413.
11. Bruno, Bonnie and Comm, Joel. *Internet Family Fun: Parents Guide to Safe Surfing.* San Francisco: No Starch Press, 1997.

SEXUAL ADDICTIONS

1 www.iProdigals.com. 888-535-5565 Has a comprehensive list of resources available.
2. www.overcomersoutreach.org. 800-310-3001.
3. www.faithfulandtrueministries.com
4. www.purelifeministries.org
5. www.pureintimacy.org
6. www.lifestrategies.org
7. www.exxit.org
8. www.stonegateresources.com
9. www.sexaddict.com
10. www.afa.net
11. www.christianrecovery.com
12. www.sexualwholeness.com

FOR KIDS WOUNDED BY FAMILIES WITH ADDICTIONS

1. www.confidentkids.com.
2. www.celebraterecovery.com. Youth division- Life Hurts/God Heals.

FOR WIVES OF SEX ADDICTS

1. www.newlifepartners.org
2. Weiss, Douglas. *Beyond Love: A 12 step Guide for Partners.* Los Angeles: Discovery Press, 1995.
3. Means, Marsha. *Living with your Husband's Secret Wars.* Grand Rapids: Revell Publishers, 1999.
4. Hall, Laurie. *An Affair of the Mind.* Colorado Springs: Focus on the Family, 1996.
5. Codependents of Sex addicts (cosa) 763-537-6904.

RESOURCES FOR ACCOUNTABILITY PARTNERS

1. Weiss, Douglass. *101 Practical Exercises: A Christian Guide for Sex Addiction Recovery.* Order from Heart to Heart Counseling P.O. Box 51055 Colorado Springs, CO www.sexaddict.com. 710-278-3708.

BOOKS FOR SEXUAL ADDICTION

1. Arterburn, Stephen. *Addicted to Love*. Dover: Vine Books, 1991.
2. Arterburn, Stephen; Stoeker, Fred; Yorkey, Mike. *Every Man's Battle.* New York: Waterbrook Press, 2000.
3. Carnes, Patrick. *Out of the Shadows: Understanding Sexual Addiction*. Minneapolis: Compcare Publications,1983.
4. Daniels, Robert. *The War Within: Gaining Victory over the Battle for Sexual Purity.* Wheaton: Crossway Books, 1997.
5. Earle, Ralph and Crow, Gregory. *Lonely All the Time: Recognizing, Understanding and Overcoming Sex Addiction for Addicts and Codependents.* Blaine: Tristar, 1998.

6. Laaser, Mark. *Faithful and True: Sexual Integrity in a Fallen World.* Grand Rapids: Zondervan, 1992.
7. Schaumburg, Harry. *False Intimacy: Understanding the Struggle of Sexual Addiction. Colorado Springs:* NavPress, 1997.
8. Willingham, Russell. *Breaking Free: Understanding Sexual Addiction and the Healing Power of Jesus.* Downers Grove: Intervarsity Press,1999.

GENERAL CHRISTIAN WEBSITES

1. www.family.org (Focus on the Family)
2. www.gospelcom.net (Internet for Christians)
3. www.christcom.net
4. www.cybergrace.com
5. www.christianity.net
6. www.crosssearch.com (Directory to 8000 Christian links)
7. www.christianitytoday.com
8. www.nauticom.net
9. www.familyeducation.com
10. www.crown.org (Larry Burkett's Financial ministry website)
11. www.aacc.net (American Association of Christian Counselors)
12. www.abstinence.net
13. www.josh.org (Josh McDowell's database of information)

PARENTING WEBSITES

1. www.family.org
2. www.positiveparenting.com
3. www.parentsplace.com
4. www.peggiesplace.com
5. www.parenttalk.com
6. www.familylifetoday.com
7. www.youthwalk.org

INTERNET FILTERS

1. Cyberpatrol; info@microsys.com www.microsys.com. 800-828-2608.
2. Cybersitter; www.cybersitter.com. 800-388-2761.
3. Surfwatch; www.surfwatch.com/home.
4. www.new-life.net (Good general review of filters and ISP's)

IDEAS FOR HOSTING A CHRISTIAN WEBSITE AND KEEPING CHRIST IN CYBER-SPACE

1. www.annieshomepage.com
2. www.ChristianWebHost.com

About the Author

Dr. Mary Ezzo is in private practice as a Family Physician in the Twin Cities. She is Medical Director of HealthEast Care System's Healthier Communities in St. Paul, Minnesota. She is a 1981 Graduate of Case Western Reserve Medical School. In 2000, she was the first recipient of the HealthEast Physician Community Service Award. Dr. Ezzo is a mother, stepmother and grandmother. She lives with her husband Paul and sons, David and Matthew.

About the Cover Designer

Michael Macone is a Graphic Designer who also enjoys many other facets of art. He operates a pottery shop and gallery, creates signs and banners for his church, and produces videos for commercial use and Christian ministry. He lives in Northern Wisconsin with his wife and four children.

For Information on
Scheduling a Weekend Parenting Conference
contact Mary Ezzo through Solid Foundations Publishing
P.O. Box 41
Cottage Grove, MN 55016-0041
651-458-3573